Oracle Press™

Mastering Lambdas

Join the Oracle Press Community at
OraclePressBooks.com

Find the latest information on Oracle products and technologies. Get exclusive discounts on Oracle Press books. Interact with expert Oracle Press authors and other Oracle Press Community members. Read blog posts, download content and multimedia, and so much more. Join today!

Join the Oracle Press Community today and get these benefits:

- Exclusive members-only discounts and offers

- Full access to all the features on the site: sample chapters, free code and downloads, author blogs, podcasts, videos, and more

- Interact with authors and Oracle enthusiasts

- Follow your favorite authors and topics and receive updates

- Newsletter packed with exclusive offers and discounts, sneak previews, and author podcasts and interviews

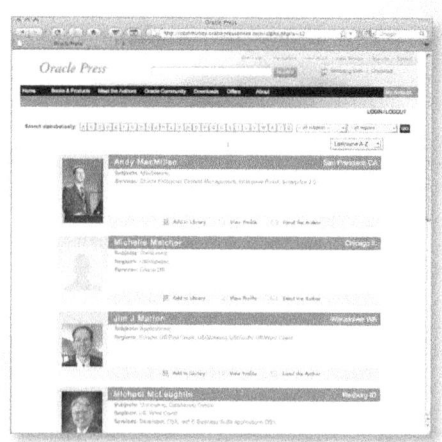

Oracle Press™

 @OraclePress

Oracle Press™

Mastering Lambdas: Java Programming in a Multicore World

Maurice Naftalin

New York   Chicago   San Francisco
Athens   London   Madrid   Mexico City   Milan
New Delhi   Singapore   Sydney   Toronto

Cataloging-in-Publication Data is on file with the Library of Congress

McGraw-Hill Education books are available at special quantity discounts to use as premiums and sales promotions, or for use in corporate training programs. To contact a representative, please visit the Contact Us pages at www.mhprofessional.com.

Mastering Lambdas: Java Programming in a Multicore World

1 2 3 4 5 6 7 8 9 0 DOC DOC 1 0 9 8 7 6 5 4

ISBN: 978-0-07-182962-5
MHID: 0-07-182962-8

Sponsoring Editor Brandi Shailer	**Technical Editors** Stuart Marks and Brian Goetz	**Production Supervisor** Jean Bodeaux
Editorial Supervisor Janet Walden	**Copy Editor** Margaret Berson	**Composition** Maurice Naftalin
Project Manager Hardik Popli, Cenveo® Publisher Services	**Proofreader** Lisa McCoy	**Illustration** Maurice Naftalin
Acquisitions Coordinator Amanda Russell	**Indexer** Jack Lewis	**Art Director, Cover** Jeff Weeks

To my boys: Joe, Isaac, Daniel, and Ben

About the Author

Maurice Naftalin has over 30 years' experience in IT as a developer, designer, architect, manager, teacher, and author. Naftalin, a certified Java programmer, has worked in every release of Java to date. His experience in Java and business gives him a unique perspective on the fundamental change that comes with introducing lambda expressions in Java SE 8. Naftalin is a frequent presenter at conferences worldwide, including the annual JavaOne. He runs a popular tutorial site in collaboration with Oracle's development team, www.lambdafaq.org, focused on the new language features in Java 8.

About the Technical Editors

Stuart Marks works on the JDK Core Libraries team in the Java Platform Group at Oracle. He is currently working on lambda, streams, and collections, as well as improving test quality and performance. He has previously worked on JavaFX and Java ME at Sun Microsystems. He has over 20 years of software platform product development experience in the areas of window systems, interactive graphics, and mobile and embedded systems. Stuart holds a master's degree in Computer Science and a bachelor's degree in Electrical Engineering from Stanford University. He lives with his wife and daughter in California.

Brian Goetz is one of the leading authorities on Java programming. He is the author of the very successful *Java Concurrency in Practice*, as well as over 75 articles on Java development. He was the specification lead for JSR-335 (Lambda Expressions for the Java Language) and has served on numerous other JCP Expert Groups. Brian is the Java Language Architect at Oracle.

Contents

Foreword

Java SE 8 may well represent the largest change ever to the Java language and libraries. Since you're reading a book called *Mastering Lambdas*, you probably already know that the biggest new feature is the addition of *lambda expressions*. Depending on your perspective, this evolution began in 2009 (when Project Lambda was launched), or 2006 (when several proposals were made for adding closures to Java), or 1997 (when inner classes were added), or 1941 (when Alonzo Church published his foundational work on the theory of computing, from which lambda expressions get their name).

However long it took to get here, it's about time! While it may initially appear that lambda expressions are "just another language feature," in reality, they will change the way you think about programming, offering a powerful new tool for applying abstraction to the programming challenges you face every day. Of course, Java already gives us powerful tools for abstraction, such as inheritance and generics, but these are largely about abstracting over *data*. Lambda expressions complement these by giving us a better tool for abstracting over *behavior*.

In embracing lambda expressions, Java has taken a mild turn towards functional programming. While it might seem that object-oriented programming and functional programming are competing disciplines, they offer us complementary tools for managing program complexity. And, as hardware parallelism continues to increase, the building blocks of functional programming—immutable values and pure functions—become even more effective tools for managing that complexity.

Mastering Lambdas: Java Programming in a Multicore World covers all the details of the new language and library features of Java SE 8—lambda expressions, default methods, and the Streams library—in a layered, disciplined fashion. Even more importantly, it connects the details of the features back to their underlying design decisions, enabling readers to get the most out of these new features by understanding the motivation and principles behind them. At the same time, it remains focused on the real payoff, which is not the features themselves, but what they enable: more expressive, more powerful, less error-prone user code. And navigating the reader to this payoff is what this book is really about.

Let *Mastering Lambdas* be your introduction to programming with this new-and-improved Java. Once you get started, I'm sure you'll be hooked!

–Brian Goetz
Java Language Architect, Oracle Corporation

Acknowledgments

I could not have written this book without unfailing help, encouragement, and feedback from people in the Oracle language team: Brian Goetz, Paul Sandoz, Aleksey Shipilev, and Dan Smith. Stuart Marks provided comments so valuable that they helped to shape the book.

I thank the people whose reviews saved me from many mistakes and often suggested new directions: Graham Allan, Maurizio Cimadore, Chris Czarnecki, John Kostaras, Kirk Pepperdine, Jeremy Prime, and Philip Wadler. Of course, any remaining errors are my responsibility alone.

I owe a huge debt to my editor, Brandi Shailer, for her endless patience and optimism during the long gestation of this project.

Introduction

The changes in Java 8 are the biggest in the history of the language. They promise to alter Java programming toward a functional style will help you to write code that is more concise and expressive, and (in many cases) ready to take advantage of parallel hardware. In this book, you will discover how the seemingly minor changes that introduce lambda expressions make this possible. You will learn how lambda expressions enable you to write a Java function in a single line of code, and how to use this capability to program the new Stream API, condensing verbose collection processing code into simple and readable stream programs. Studying the mechanisms that create and consume streams will lead to an analysis of their performance and enable you to judge when to invoke the parallel execution features of the API.

Lastly, integrating the new features into the existing Java platform libraries required the evolution of existing collection interfaces, previously prevented by compatibility problems. You will learn about how default methods solve these problems and how to use them in evolving your own APIs.

Chapter 1: Taking Java to the Next Level

This chapter sets the scene for the introduction of both lambda expressions and streams to Java, motivating the changes by the need both for better programming idioms and for Java to begin providing support for multicore processors.

Chapter 2: The Basics of Java Lambda Expressions

This chapter covers the syntax of lambda expressions, how and where you can use them, how they differ from anonymous inner classes, and the convenient shorthand provided by method and constructor references.

Chapter 3: Introduction to Streams and Pipelines

This chapter explains the stream lifecycle and the basis of programming with streams, with collection processing providing examples of stream sources and of intermediate and terminal operations.

Chapter 4: Ending Streams: Collection and Reduction

This chapter gives a detailed view of terminal operations, and in particular how stream elements can be accumulated into collections using mutable reduction. The examples of Chapter 3 are extended using collectors, the library implementations of mutable reduction. We will see when it is necessary to go beyond the library implementations and how to write your own collector.

Chapter 5: Starting Streams: Sources and Spliterators

This chapter examines ways of starting streams, both using library classes and, when necessary, writing your own spliterator. The problem of exception handling in stream programming is explored in depth. An extended example shows the flexibility of the model by reimplementing various options of grep by means of stream processing.

Chapter 6: Stream Performance

This chapter offers ways of understanding the relative performance of stream processes executing in parallel in terms of the splitting efficiency of their sources, the workload of their intermediate operations, and the concurrency of their terminal operations. Microbenchmarks are introduced as a way of measuring stream performance and, using them, the programs developed elsewhere in the book are analyzed.

Chapter 7: API Evolution with Default Methods

This chapter explains how the introduction of default methods solves long-standing problems in Java programming, and in particular how they make it possible, for the first time, for interface-based Java APIs to evolve. It also covers the use of static interface methods.

Intended Audience

This book is aimed at Java developers comfortable with any version from Java 5 onward who have heard about the exciting changes in Java 8 and want to know about them. You do not need to have met lambda expressions or closures in any other language, or to have any experience with functional programming. (If you have, so much the better, of course.)

The book doesn't assume familiarity with the platform libraries except for the standard collections of the Java Collections Framework; if you don't know them well, be prepared to consult the Javadoc sometimes.

A few sections contain more advanced material: these are introduced as being suitable for a second reading.

Examples, Feedback, and Further Study

Code used in this book can be downloaded from the Oracle Press website at www.OraclePressBooks.com. Source code and errata will also be posted to the book's product page on www.mhprofessional.com. Simply search by ISBN and download the necessary files.

Visit the book's website at www.masteringlambdas.org for discussion, links to further study, or to contact the author.

CHAPTER

1

Taking Java to
the Next Level

T he changes in Java 8 are the biggest in the history of the language, combining coordinated changes to the language, the libraries, and the virtual machine. They promise to alter the way we think about the execution of Java programs and to make the language fit for use in a world, soon to arrive, of massively parallel hardware. Yet for such an important innovation, the actual changes to the language seem quite minor. What is it about these apparently minor modifications that will make such a big difference? And why should we change a programming model that has served us so well throughout the lifetime of Java, and indeed for much longer before that? In this chapter we will explore some of the limitations of that model and see how the lambda-related features of Java 8 will enable Java to evolve to meet the challenges of a new generation of hardware architectures.

1.1 From External to Internal Iteration

Let's start with code that simply iterates over a collection of mutable objects, calling a single method on each of them. The following code fragment constructs a collection of `java.awt.Point` objects (`Point` is a conveniently simple library class, consisting only of a pair (x,y) of coordinates). Our code then iterates over the collection, translating (i.e., moving) each `Point` by a distance of 1 on both the x and y axes.

```
List<Point> pointList = Arrays.asList(new Point(1, 2), new Point(2, 3));
for (Point p : pointList) {
    p.translate(1, 1);
}
```

Before Java 5 introduced the for-each loop, we would have written the loop like this:

```
for (Iterator pointItr = pointList.iterator(); pointItr.hasNext(); ) {
    ((Point) pointItr.next()).translate(1, 1);
}
```

Or, in a clearer idiom (though less favored because it increases the scope of pointItr):

```
Iterator pointItr = pointList.iterator();
while (pointItr.hasNext()) {
    ((Point) pointItr.next()).translate(1, 1);
}
```

Here we are asking `pointList` to create an `Iterator` object on our behalf, and we are then using that object to access the elements of `pointList` in turn. This version is still relevant, because today this is the code that the Java compiler generates to implement the for-each loop. Its key aspect for us is that the order of access to the elements of `pointList` is controlled by the `Iterator`—there is nothing that we can do to change it. The `Iterator` for an `ArrayList`, for example, will return the elements of the list in sequential order.

Why is this problematic? After all, when the Java Collections Framework was designed in 1998, it seemed perfectly reasonable to dictate the access order of list elements in this way. What has changed since then?

Part of the answer lies in how hardware has been evolving. Workstations and servers have been equipped with multiple processors for a long time, but between the design of the Java Collections Framework in 1998 and the appearance of the first dual-core processors in personal computers in 2005, a revolution had taken place in chip design. A 40-year trend of exponentially increasing processor speed had been halted by inescapable physical facts: signal leakage, inadequate heat dissipation, and the hard truth that, even at the speed of light, data cannot cross a chip quickly enough for further processor speed increases.

But clock speed limitations notwithstanding, the density of chip components continued to increase. So, since it wasn't possible to offer a 6 GHz core, the chip vendors instead began to offer dual-core processors, each core running at 3 GHz. This trend has continued, with currently no end in sight; at the time of the Java 8 ship date (March 2014) quad-core processors have become mainstream, eight-core processors are appearing in the commodity hardware market, and specialist servers have long been available with dozens of cores per processor. The direction is clear, and any programming model that doesn't adapt to it will fail in the face of competition from models that do adapt. Adaptation would mean providing developers with an accessible way of making use of the processing power of multiple cores by distributing tasks over them to be executed in parallel.[1] Failing to adapt, on the other hand, would mean that Java programs, bound by default to a single core, would run at a progressively greater speed disadvantage compared to programs in languages that had found ways to assist users in easily parallelizing their code.

The need for change is shown by the code at the start of this section, which could only access list elements one at a time in the order dictated by the iterator. Collection processing is not the only processor-intensive task that programs have to carry out, but it is one of the most important. The model of iteration embodied in Java's loop constructs forces collection element processing into a serial straitjacket, and that is a serious problem at a time when the most pressing requirement for runtimes—at least as far as performance is concerned—is precisely the opposite: to distribute processing over multiple cores. Although we will see in Chapter 6 that by no means every problem will benefit from parallelization, the best cases give us speedup that is nearly linear in the number of cores.

---

[1] The distribution of a processing task over multiple processors is often called *parallelization*. Even if we dislike this word, it's a useful shorthand that will sometimes make explanations shorter and more readable.

1.1.1 Internal Iteration

The intrusiveness of the serial model of iteration becomes obvious when we imagine imposing it on a real-world situation. If someone were to ask you to mail some letters with the instruction "repeat the following action: if you have any more letters, take the next one in alphabetical order of addressee's surname and put it in the mailbox," your kindest thought would probably be that they have overspecified the task. You would know that ordering doesn't matter in this task, and neither does the mode—sequential or parallel—of execution, yet it would seem you aren't allowed to ignore them. In this situation you might feel some sympathy with a collection forced by external iteration to process elements serially and in a fixed order when much better strategies may be available.

In reality, all you need to know for that real-world task is that every letter in a bundle needs mailing; exactly how to do that should be up to you. And in the same way, we ought to be able to tell collections *what* should be done to each element they contain, rather than specifying *how*, as external iteration does. If we could do that, what would the code look like? Collections would have to expose a method accepting the "what," namely the task to be executed on each element; an obvious name for this method is forEach. With it, we can imagine replacing the iterative code from the start of this section with this:

```
pointList.forEach(/*translate the point by (1,1)*/);
```

Before Java 8 this would have been a strange suggestion, since java.util.List (which is the type of pointList) has no forEach method and, as an interface, cannot have one added. However, in Chapter 7 we'll see that Java 8 overcomes this problem with the introduction of non-abstract interface methods.

The new method Collection.forEach (actually inherited by Collection from its superinterface Iterable) is an example of *internal iteration*, so called because, although the explicit iterative code is no longer obvious, iteration is still taking place internally. It is now managed by the forEach method, which applies its *behavioral parameter* to each element of its collection.

The change from external to internal iteration may seem a small one, simply a matter of moving the work of iteration across the client-library boundary. But the consequences are not small. The parallelization work that we require can now be defined in the collection class instead of repeatedly in every client method that must iterate over the collection. Moreover, the implementation is free to use additional techniques such as laziness and out-of-order execution—and, indeed, others yet to be discovered—to get to the answer faster.

So internal iteration is necessary if a programming model is to allow collection library writers the freedom to choose, for each collection, the best way of implementing bulk processing. But what is to replace the comment in the call of forEach—how can the collection's methods be told what task is to be executed on each element?

1.1.2 The Command Pattern

There's no need to go outside traditional Java mechanisms to find an answer to this question. For example, we routinely create `Runnable` instances and pass them as arguments. If you think of a `Runnable` as an object representing a task to be executed when its `run` method is called, you can see that what we now require is very similar. For another example, the Swing framework allows the developer to define an action that will be executed in response to a number of different events—menu item selection, button press, etc.—on the user interface. If you are familiar with classical design patterns, you will recognize this loose description of the Command Pattern.

In the case we're considering, what command is needed? Our starting point was a call to the `translate` method of every `Point` in a `List`. So for this example, it appears that `forEach` should accept as its argument an object exposing a method that will call `translate` on each element of the list. If we make this object an instance of a more general interface, `PointAction` say, then we can define different implementations of `PointAction` for different actions that we want to have iteratively executed on `Point` collections:

```
public interface PointAction {
    void doForPoint(Point p);
}
```

Right now, the implementation we want is

```
class TranslateByOne implements PointAction {
    public void doForPoint(Point p) {
        p.translate(1, 1);
    }
}
```

Now we can sketch a naïve implementation of `forEach`:

```
public class PointArrayList extends ArrayList<Point> {
    public void forEach(PointAction t) {
        for (Point p : this) {
            t.doForPoint(p);
        }
    }
}
```

and if we make `pointList` an instance of `PointArrayList`, our goal of internal iteration is achieved with this client code:

```
pointList.forEach(new TranslateByOne());
```

Of course, this toy code is absurdly specialized; we aren't really going to write a new interface for every element type we need to work with. Fortunately, we don't need to; there is nothing special about the names `PointAction` and `doForPoint`; if we simply replace them consistently with other names, nothing changes. In the Java 8 collections library they are called `Consumer` and `accept`. So our `PointAction` interface becomes:

```
public interface Consumer<T> {
    void accept(T t);
}
```

Parameterizing the type of the interface allows us to dispense with the specialized `ArrayList` subclass and instead add the method `forEach` directly to the class itself, as is done by inheritance in Java 8. This method takes a `java.util.function.Consumer`, which will receive and process each element of the collection.

```
public class ArrayList<E> {
    ...
    public void forEach(Consumer<E> c) {
        for (E e : this) {
            c.accept(e);
        }
    }
}
```

Applying these changes to the client code, we get

```
class TranslateByOne implements Consumer<Point> {
    public void accept(Point p) {
        p.translate(1, 1);
    }
}
...
pointList.forEach(new TranslateByOne());
```

You may think that this code is still pretty clumsy. But notice that the clumsiness is now concentrated in the representation of each command by an instance of a class. In many cases, this is overkill. In the present case, for example, all that `forEach` really needs is the *behavior* of the single method `accept` of the object that has been supplied to it. State and all the other apparatus that make up the object are included only because method arguments in Java, if not primitives, have to be object references. But we have always needed to specify this apparatus—until now.

1.1.3 Lambda Expressions

The code that concluded the previous section is not idiomatic Java for the command pattern. When, as in this case, a class is both small and unlikely to be reused, a more common usage is to define an *anonymous inner class*:

```
pointList.forEach(new Consumer<Point>() {
    public void accept(Point p) {
        p.translate(1, 1);
    }
});
```

Experienced Java developers are so accustomed to seeing code like this that we have often forgotten how we felt when we first encountered it. Common first reactions to the syntax for anonymous inner classes used in this way are that it is ugly, verbose, and difficult to understand quickly, even though all it is really doing is to say "do this for each element." You don't have to agree completely with these judgements to accept that any attempt to persuade developers to rely on this idiom for every collection operation is unlikely to be very successful. And this, at last, is our cue for the introduction of lambda expressions.[2]

To reduce the verbosity of this call, we should try to identify those places where we are supplying information that the compiler could instead infer from the context. One such piece of information is the name of the interface being implemented by the anonymous inner class. It's enough for the compiler to know that the declared type of the parameter to `forEach` is `Consumer<T>`; that is sufficient information to allow the supplied argument to be checked for type compatibility. Let's de-emphasize the code that the compiler can infer:

```
pointList.forEach(new Consumer<Point>() {
    public void accept(Point p) {
        p.translate(1, 1);
    }
});
```

Second, what about the name of the method being overridden—in this case, `accept`? There's no way that the compiler can infer that in general. But in the case of `Consumer` there is no need to infer the name, because the interface has only a single method. This "one method interface" pattern is so useful for defining callbacks that it has an official status: any object to be used in the abbreviated form that we are developing must implement an interface like this, exposing a single abstract method (this is called

---

[2] People are often curious about the origin of the name. The idea of lambda expressions comes from a model of computation developed in the 1930s by the American mathematician Alonzo Church, in which the Greek letter λ (lambda) represents functional abstraction. But why that particular letter? Church seems to have liked to tease: asked about his choice, his usual explanation involved accidents of typesetting, but in later years he had an alternative answer: "Eeny, meeny, miny, moe."

a *functional interface*, or sometimes a *SAM* interface). That gives the compiler a way to choose the correct method without ambiguity. Again let's de-emphasize the code that can be inferred in this way:

```
pointList.forEach(new Consumer<Point>() {
    public void accept(Point p) {
        p.translate(1, 1);
    }
});
```

Finally, the instantiated type of `Consumer` can often be inferred from the context, in this case from the fact that when the `forEach` method calls `accept`, it supplies it with an element of `pointList`, previously declared as a `List<Point>`. That identifies the type parameter to `Consumer` as `Point`, allowing us to omit the explicit type declaration of the argument to `accept`.

This is what's left when we de-emphasize this last component of the `forEach` call:

```
pointList.forEach(new Consumer<Point>() {
    public void accept(Point p) {
        p.translate(1, 1);
    }
});
```

The argument to `forEach` represents an object, implementing the interface (`Consumer`) required by `forEach`, such that when `accept` (the only abstract method on that interface) is called for a `pointList` element `p`, the effect will be to call `p.translate(1, 1)`.

Some extra syntax ("`->`") is required to separate the *parameter list* from the *expression body*. With that addition, we finally get the simple form for a lambda expression. Here it is, being used in internal iteration:

```
pointList.forEach(p -> p.translate(1, 1));
```

If you are unused to reading lambda expressions, you may find it helpful for the moment to continue to think of them as an abbreviation for a method declaration, mentally mapping the parameter list of the lambda to that of the imaginary method, and its body (often preceded by an added `return`) to the method body. In the next chapter, we will see that it is going to be necessary to vary the simple syntax of the preceding example for lambda expressions with multiple parameters and with more elaborate bodies and in cases where the compiler cannot infer parameter types. But if you have followed the reasoning that brought us to this point, you should have a basic understanding of the motivation for the introduction of lambda expressions and of the form that they have taken.

This section has covered a lot of ground. To summarize: we began by considering the adaptations that our programming model needs to make in order to accommodate the requirements of changing hardware architectures; this brought us to a review of processing of collection elements, which in turn made us aware of the need to have a concise way of defining behavior for collections to execute; finally, paring away the excess text from anonymous inner class definitions brought us to a simple syntax for lambda expressions.

In the remaining sections of this chapter, we will look at some of the new idioms that lambda expressions make possible. We will see that bulk processing of collection elements can be written in a much more expressive style, that these changes in idiom make it much easier for library writers to incorporate parallel algorithms to take advantage of new hardware architectures, and finally that emphasizing functional behavior can improve the design of APIs. It's an impressive list of achievements for such an innocuous-looking change!

1.2 From Collections to Streams

Let's extend the example of the previous section a little. In real-life programs, it's common to process collections in a number of stages: a collection is iteratively processed to produce a new collection, which in turn is iteratively processed, and so on. Here is an example—rather artificial, in the interests of simplicity—which starts with a collection of `Integer` instances, then applies an arbitrary transformation to produce a collection of `Point` instances, and finally finds the maximum among the distances of each `Point` from the origin.

```
List<Integer> intList = Arrays.asList(1, 2, 3, 4, 5);
List<Point> pointList = new ArrayList<>();
for (Integer i : intList) {
    pointList.add(new Point(i % 3, i / 1));
}
double maxDistance = Double.MIN_VALUE;
for (Point p : pointList) {
    maxDistance = Math.max(p.distance(0, 0), maxDistance);
}
```

Although it could certainly be improved, this is idiomatic Java—most developers have seen many examples of code in this pattern—but if we look at it with fresh eyes, some unpleasant features stand out at once. Firstly, it is very verbose, taking nine lines of code to carry out only three operations. Secondly, the collection `pointList`, required only as intermediate storage, is an overhead on the operation of the program; if the intermediate storage is very large, creating it would at best add to garbage collection overheads, and at worst would exhaust available heap space. Thirdly, there is

an implicit assumption, difficult to spot, that the minimum value of an empty list is
`Double.MIN_VALUE`. But the worst aspect of all is the gap between the developer's in-
tentions and the way that they are expressed in code. To understand this program, you
have to work out what it's doing, then guess the developer's intention (or, if you're very
fortunate, read the comments), and only then check its correctness by matching the
operation of the program to the informal specification you deduced.[3] All this work is
slow and error-prone—indeed, the very purpose of a high-level language is supposed
to be to minimize it by supporting code that is as close as possible to the developer's
mental model. So how can the gap be closed?

Let's restate the problem specification:

> "Apply a transformation to each one of a collection of `Integer` instances
> to produce a `Point`, then find the greatest distance of any of these `Points`
> from the origin."

If we de-emphasize the parts of the preceding code that do not correspond to the
elements of this informal specification, we see what a poor match there is between
code and problem specification. Omitting the first line, in which the list `intList` is
initially created, we get:

```
List<Point> pointList = new ArrayList<>();
for (Integer i : intList) {
    pointList.add(new Point(i % 3, i / 3));
}
double maxDistance = Double.MIN_VALUE;
for (Point p : pointList) {
    maxDistance = Math.max(p.distance(0, 0), maxDistance);
}
```

This suggests a new, data-oriented way of looking at the program, one that will
look familiar if you are used to Unix pipes and filters: we can follow the progress of
a single value from the source collection, viewing it as being transformed first from
an `Integer` to a `Point` and second from a `Point` to a `double`. Both of these transformations can take place in isolation, without any reference to the other values being
processed—exactly the requirement for parallelization. Only with the third step, finding the greatest distance, is it necessary for the values to interact (and even then, there
are techniques for efficiently computing this in parallel).

This data-oriented view can be represented diagrammatically, as in Figure 1-1. In
this figure it is clear that the rectangular boxes represent operations. The connecting

---

[3] The situation is better than it used to be. Some of us are old enough to remember how much of this
kind of work was involved in writing big programs in assembler (*really* low-level languages, not far removed
from machine code). Programming languages have become much more expressive since then, but there is
still plenty of room for progress.

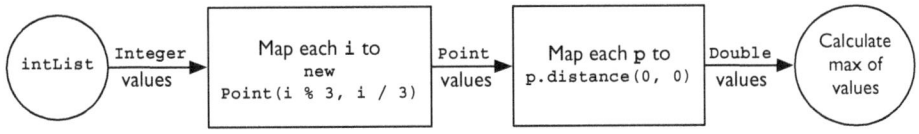

FIGURE 1-1. *Composing streams into a data pipeline*

lines represent something new, a way of delivering a sequence of values to an operation. This is different from any kind of collection, because at a given moment the values to be delivered by a connector may not all have been generated yet. These value sequences are called *streams*. Streams differ from collections in that they provide an (optionally) ordered sequence of values without providing any storage for those values; they are "data in motion," a means for expressing bulk data operations. If the idea of streams is new to you, it may help to imagine a kind of iterator on which the only operation is like next, except that besides returning the next value, it can signal that there are no more values to get. In the Java 8 collections API, streams are represented by interfaces—Stream for reference values, and IntStream, LongStream, and DoubleStream for streams of primitive values—in the package java.util.stream.

In this view, the operations represented by the boxes in Figure 1-1 are operations on streams. The boxes in this figure represent two applications of an operation called map; it transforms each stream element using a systematic rule. Looking at map alone, we might think that we were dealing with operations on individual stream elements. But we will soon meet other stream operations that can reorder, drop, or even insert values; each of these operations can be described as taking a stream and transforming it in some way. Each rectangular box represents an *intermediate operation*, one that is not only defined on a stream, but that also returns a stream as its output. For example, assuming for a moment that a stream intStream forms the input to the first operation, the transformations made by the intermediate operations of Figure 1-1 can be represented in code as:

```
Stream<Point> points = intStream.map(i -> new Point(i % 3, i / 3));
DoubleStream distances = points.mapToDouble(p -> p.distance(0, 0));
```

The circle at the end of the pipeline represents the *terminal operation* max. Terminal operations consume a stream, optionally returning a single value, or—if the stream is empty—nothing, represented by an empty Optional or one of its specializations (see p. 65):

```
OptionalDouble maxDistance = distances.max();
```

Pipelines like that in Figure 1-1 have a beginning, a middle, and an end. We have seen the operations that defined the middle and the end; what about the beginning? The values flowing into streams can be supplied by a variety of sources—collections, arrays, or generating functions. In practice, a common use case will be feeding the contents of a collection into a stream, as here. Java 8 collections expose a new method `stream()` for this purpose, so the start of the pipeline can be represented as:

```
Stream<Integer> intStream = intList.stream();
```

And the complete code with which this section began has become:

```
OptionalDouble maxDistance =
    intList.stream()
        .map(i -> new Point(i % 3, i / 3))
        .mapToDouble(p -> p.distance(0, 0))
        .max();
```

This style, often called *fluent* because "the code flows," is unfamiliar in the context of collection processing and may seem initially difficult to read in this context. However, compared to the successive iterations in the code that introduced this section, it provides a nice balance of conciseness with a close correspondence to the problem statement: "map each integer in the source `intList` to a corresponding `Point`, map each `Point` in the resulting list to its distance from the origin, then find the maximum of the resulting values." The structure of the code highlights the key operations, rather than obscuring them as in the original.

As a bonus, the performance overhead of creating and managing intermediate collections has disappeared as well: executed sequentially, the stream code is more than twice as fast as the loop version. Executed in parallel, virtually perfect speedup is achieved on large data sets (for more details of the experiment, see p. 148).

1.3 From Sequential to Parallel

This chapter began with the assertion that Java now needs to support parallel processing of collections, and that lambdas are an essential step in providing this support. We've come most of the way by seeing how lambdas make it easy for client code developers to make use of internal iteration. The last step is to see how internal iteration of the collection classes actually implements parallelism. It's useful to know the principles of how this will work, although you don't need them for everyday use—the complexity of the implementations is well hidden from developers of client code.

Independent execution on multiple cores is accomplished by assigning a different thread to each core, each thread executing a subtask of the work to be done—in this case, a subset of the collection elements to be processed. For example, given a four-core processor and a list of N elements, a program might define a `solve` algorithm to break the task down for parallel execution in the following way:

```
if the task list contains more than N/4 elements {
    leftTask = task.getLeftHalf()
    rightTask = task.getRightHalf()
    doInParallel {
        leftResult = leftTask.solve()
        rightResult = rightTask.solve()
    }
    result = combine(leftResult, rightResult)
} else {
    result = task.solveSequentially()
}
```

The preceding pseudocode is a highly simplified description of parallel processing using a list specialization of the pattern of *recursive decomposition*—recursively splitting large tasks into smaller ones, to be executed in parallel, until the subtasks are "small enough" to be executed in serial. Implementing recursive decomposition requires knowing how to split tasks in this way, how to execute sufficiently small ones without further splitting, and how to then combine the results of these smaller executions. The technique for splitting depends on the source of the data; in this case, splitting a list has an obvious implementation. Combining the results of subtasks is often achieved by applying the pipeline terminal operation to them; for the example of this chapter, it involves taking the maximum of two subtask results.

The Java fork/join framework uses this pattern, allocating threads from its pool to new subtasks rather than creating new ones. Clearly, reimplementing this pattern is far more coding work than can realistically be expected of developers every time a collection is to be processed. This is library work—or it certainly should be!

In this case, the library class is the collection; from Java 8 onward, the collections library classes will be able to use the fork/join framework in this way, so that client developers can put parallelization, essentially a performance issue, to the back of their minds and get on with solving business problems. For our current example, the only change necessary to the client code is emphasized here:

```
OptionalDouble maxDistance =
    intList.parallelStream()
        .map(i -> new Point(i % 3, i / 3))
        .mapToDouble(p -> p.distance(0, 0))
        .max();
```

This illustrates what is meant by the slogan for the introduction of parallelism in Java 8: *explicit but unobtrusive*. Parallel execution is achieved by breaking the initial list of `Integer` values down recursively, as in the pseudocode for `solve`, until the

sublists are small enough, then executing the entire pipeline serially, and finally combining the results with max. The process for deciding what is "small enough" takes
into account the number of cores available and, sometimes, characteristics of the list.
Figure 1-2 shows the decomposition of a list for processing by four cores: in this case,
"small enough" is just the list size divided by four. (A connected problem is deciding
when a list is "big enough" to make it worthwhile to incur the overhead of executing
in parallel. Chapter 6 will explore this problem in detail.)

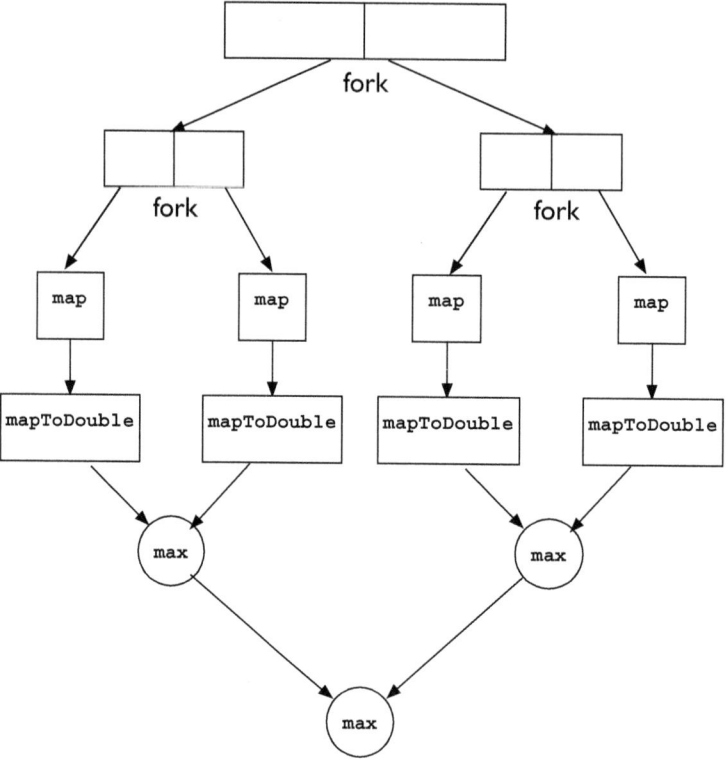

FIGURE 1-2.   *Recursive decomposition of a list processing task*

Unobtrusive parallelism is an example of one of the key themes of Java 8; the API
changes that it enables give much greater freedom to library developers. One important way in which they can use it is to explore the many opportunities for performance
improvement that are provided by modern—and future—machine architectures.

1.4 Composing Behaviors

Earlier in this chapter we saw how functionally similar lambda expressions are to anonymous inner classes. But writing them so differently leads to different ways of thinking about them. Lambda expressions *look* like functions, so it's natural to ask whether we can make them *behave* like functions. That change of perspective will encourage us to think about working with behaviors rather than objects, and that in turn will lead in the direction of some very different programming idioms and library APIs.

For example, a core operation on functions is *composition*: combining together two functions to make a third, whose effect is the same as applying its two components in succession. Composition is not an idea that arises at all naturally in connection with anonymous inner classes, but in a generalized form it corresponds very well to the construction of traditional object-oriented programs. And just as object-oriented programs are broken down by decomposition, the reverse of composition will work for functions too.

Suppose, for example, that we want to sort a list of `Point` instances in order of their x coordinate. The standard Java idiom for a "custom" sort[4] is to create a `Comparator`:

```
Comparator<Point> byX = new Comparator<Point>(){
    public int compare(Point p1, Point p2) {
        return Double.compare(p1.getX(), p2.getX());
    }
};
```

Substituting a lambda expression for the anonymous inner class declaration, as described in the previous section, improves the readability of the code:

```
Comparator<Point> byX =
    (p1, p2) -> Double.compare(p1.getX(), p2.getX());                ❶
```

But that doesn't help with another very significant problem: `Comparator` is mono-lithic. If we wanted to define a `Comparator` that compared on y instead of x coordi-nates, we would have to copy the entire declaration, substituting `getY` for `getX` every-where. Good programming practice should lead us to look for a better solution, and a moment's reflection shows that `Comparator` is actually carrying out two functions—extracting sort keys from its arguments and then comparing those keys. We should be able to improve the code of ❶ by building a `Comparator` function parameterized on these two components. We'll now evolve the code to do that. The intermediate stages may seem awkward and verbose, but persist: the conclusion will be worthwhile.

---

[4] Two ways of comparing and sorting objects are standard in the Java platform: a class can have a *natural order*; in this case, it implements the interface `Comparable` and so exposes a `compareTo` method that an object can use to compare itself with another. Or a `Comparator` can be created for the purpose, as in this case.

To start, let's turn the two concrete component functions that we have into lambda form. We know the type of the functional interface for the key extractor function—`Comparator`—but we also need the type of the functional interface corresponding to the function `p -> p.getX()`. Looking in the package devoted to the declaration of functional interfaces, `java.util.function`, we find the interface `Function`:

```
public interface Function<T,R> {
    public R apply(T t);
}
```

So we can now write the lambda expressions for both key extraction and key comparison:

```
Function<Point,Double> keyExtractor = p -> p.getX();
Comparator<Double> keyComparer = (d1, d2) -> Double.compare(d1, d2);
```

And our version of `Comparator<Point>` can be reassembled from these two smaller functions:

```
Comparator<Point> compareByX = (p1, p2) -> keyComparer.compare(
    keyExtractor.apply(p1), keyExtractor.apply(p2));                    ❷
```

This matches the form of ❶ but represents an important improvement (one that would be much more significant in a larger example): you could plug in any `keyComparer` or `keyExtractor` that had previously been defined. After all, that was the whole purpose of seeking to parameterize the larger function on its smaller components.

But although recasting the `Comparator` in this way has improved its structure, we have lost the conciseness of ❶. We can recover that in the special but very common case where `keyComparer` expresses the natural ordering on the extracted keys. Then ❷ can be rewritten as:

```
Comparator<Point> compareByX = (p1, p2) ->
    keyExtractor.apply(p1).compareTo(keyExtractor.apply(p2));           ❸
```

And, noticing the importance of this special case, the platform library designers added a static method `comparing` to the interface `Comparator`; given a key extractor, it creates the corresponding `Comparator`[5] using natural ordering on the keys. Here is its method declaration, in which generic type parameters have been simplified for this explanation:

```
public static <T,U extends Comparable<U>>
                Comparator<T> comparing(Function<T,U> keyExtractor) {
```

---

[5] Other overloads of `comparing` can create `Comparator`s for primitive types in the same way, but since natural ordering can't be used, they instead use the `compare` methods exposed by the wrapper classes.

```
    return (c1, c2) ->
        keyExtractor.apply(c1).compareTo(keyExtractor.apply(c2));
}
```

Using that method allows us to write the following (assuming a static import declaration of `Comparators.comparing`) instead of ❸:

```
Comparator<Point> compareByX = comparing(p -> p.getX());
```
❹

Compared to ❶, ❹ is a big improvement: more concise and more immediately understandable because it isolates and lays emphasis on the important element, the key extractor, in a way that is possible only because `comparing` accepts a simple behavior and uses it to build a more complex one from it.

To see the improvement in action, imagine that our problem changes slightly so that instead of finding the single point that is furthest from the origin, we decide to print all the points in ascending order of their distance. It is straightforward to capture the necessary ordering:

```
Comparator<Point> byDistance = comparing(p -> p.distance(0, 0));
```

And to implement the changed problem specification, the stream pipeline needs only a small corresponding change:

```
intList.stream()
    .map(i -> new Point(i % 3, i / 3))
    .sorted(comparing(p -> p.distance(0, 0)))
    .forEach(p -> System.out.printf("(%f, %f)", p.getX(), p.getY()));
```

The change needed to accommodate the new problem statement illustrates some of the advantages that lambdas will bring. Changing the `Comparator` was straightforward because it is being created by composition and we needed to specify only the single component being changed. The use of the new comparator fits smoothly with the existing stream operations, and the new code is again close to the problem statement, with a clear correspondence between the changed part of the problem and the changed part of the code.

1.5 Conclusion

It should be clear by now why the introduction of lambda expressions has been so keenly awaited. In the earlier sections of this chapter we saw the possibilities they will create for performance improvement, by allowing library developers to enable automatic parallelization. Although this improvement will not be universally available— one purpose of this book is to help you to understand exactly when your application will benefit from "going parallel"—it represents a major step in the right direction, of starting to make the improved performance of modern hardware accessible to the application programmer.

In the last section, we saw how lambdas will encourage the writing of better APIs. The signature of `Comparator.comparing` is a sign of things to come: as client programmers become comfortable with supplying behaviors like the key extraction function that `comparing` accepts, fine-grained library methods like `comparing` will become the norm and, with them, corresponding improvements in the style and ease of client coding.

CHAPTER

2

The Basics of Java
Lambda Expressions

C hapter 1 gave an informal introduction to lambda expressions and motivated their introduction to Java. This chapter defines more precisely what lambda expressions are, and how and where they can be used in Java programs.

2.1 What Is a Lambda Expression?

In mathematics and computing generally, a lambda expression is a *function*: for some or all combinations of input values it specifies an output value. Until now, there has been no way to write a freestanding function in Java. Methods have often been used to stand in for functions, but always as part of an object or a class. Lambda expressions now provide a closer approach to the idea of freestanding functions.[1] In conventional Java terms, lambdas can be understood as a kind of anonymous method with a more compact syntax that also allows the omission of modifiers, return type, `throws` clause, and in some cases parameter types as well.

2.1.1 The Syntax of Lambdas

A lambda expression in Java consists of a *parameter list* separated from a *body* by a function arrow: "`->`". The examples of Chapter 1 all had a single parameter:

```
p -> p.translate(1, 1)
i -> new Point(i, i + 1)
```

But, as you would expect from the similarity to method declarations, lambdas can in general have any number of parameters. Except for lambdas that have a single parameter, like those we have seen, parameter lists must be surrounded by parentheses:

```
(x, y) -> x + y
() -> 23
```

Also, until now, parameters have been declared without being given explicit types, because lambdas are often more readable without them. It is always permissible, however, to supply parameter types—and sometimes it is necessary, when the compiler cannot infer them from the context. If you supply any types explicitly, you must supply all of them, and the parameter list must be enclosed in parentheses:

```
(int x, int y) -> x + y
```

Such explicitly typed parameters can be modified in the same way as method parameters—for example, they can be declared `final`—and annotated.

---

[1] One common question about lambdas concerns whether they are objects as traditionally defined in Java. This question has no simple answer, because although lambda expressions do currently evaluate to object references, they don't behave like objects in all respects—see, for example, §2.2.1.

The lambda body on the right-hand side of the function arrow can be an expression, as in all the examples seen so far. (Notice that method calls are expressions, including those that return `void`.) Lambdas like these are sometimes called "expression lambdas." A more general form is the "statement lambda," in which the body is a block—that is, a sequence of statements surrounded by braces:

```
(Thread t) -> { t.start(); }
() -> { System.gc(); return 0; }
```

An expression lambda

```
args -> expr
```

can be seen as a short form of the corresponding statement lambda

```
args -> { return expr; }
```

The rules for using or omitting the `return` keyword in a block body are the same as those for an ordinary method body—that is, `return` is required whenever an expression within the body is to return a value, or can instead be used without an argument to terminate execution of the body immediately. If the lambda returns `void`, then `return` may be omitted or used without an argument.

Lambda expressions are neither required nor allowed to use a `throws` clause to declare the exceptions they might throw.

2.2 Lambdas vs. Anonymous Inner Classes

If you followed the progressive transformation in Chapter 1 of an anonymous inner class into a lambda expression, you may be wondering whether, aside from concrete syntax, there is any real difference between the two. Indeed, lambda expressions are sometimes incorrectly called "syntactic sugar" for anonymous inner classes, implying that there is a simple syntactic transformation between the two. In fact, there are a number of significant differences; two in particular are important to the programmer:

1. An inner class creation expression is *guaranteed* to create a new object with unique identity, while the result of evaluating a lambda expression may or may not have unique identity, depending on the implementation. This flexibility allows the platform to use more efficient implementation strategies than for the corresponding inner classes.

2. An inner class declaration creates a new naming scope, within which `this` and `super` refer to the current instance of the inner class itself; by contrast, lambda expressions do not introduce any new naming environment. In this way they avoid the complexity in name lookup for inner classes that causes many subtle

errors, such as mistakenly calling `Object` methods on the inner class instance when the enclosing instance was intended.

These points are explained further in the next two subsections.

2.2.1 No Identity Crisis

Until now, behavior in a Java program has been associated with an object, characterized by identity, state, and behavior. Lambdas are a departure from this rule; although they share some of the properties of objects, their only use is to represent behavior. Since they have no state, the question of their identity is unimportant. The language specification explicitly leaves it undetermined, the only requirement being that a lambda must evaluate to an instance of a class that implements the appropriate functional interface (§2.4). The intention is to give the platform flexibility to optimize in ways that would not be possible if every lambda expression were required to have a unique identity.

2.2.2 Scoping Rules for Lambdas

The scoping rules for anonymous inner classes, like those for most inner classes, are complicated by the fact that they can refer both to names inherited from their supertypes and to names declared in their enclosing class. Lambda expressions are simpler, because they do not inherit names from their supertypes.[2] Other than its parameters, names used in the body of a lambda expression mean exactly the same as they do outside the body. So, for example, it is illegal to redeclare a local variable within a lambda:

```
void foo() { final int i = 2; Runnable r = () -> { int i = 3;}} // illegal
```

Parameters are like local declarations in that they may introduce new names:

```
IntUnaryOperator iuo = i -> { int j = 3; return i + j; };
```

Lambda parameters and lambda body local declarations may shadow field names (i.e., a field name can be temporarily redeclared as a parameter or local variable name).

```
class Foo {
    Object i, j;
    IntUnaryOperator iuo = i -> { int j = 3; return i + j; }
}
```

---

[2] The effect of this rule is to exclude from the scope of a lambda any declarations in its supertype (i.e., its functional interface). Interfaces can declare—besides abstract methods—static final fields, static nested classes, and default methods (see Chapter 7). None of these are in scope for an implementing lambda.

Since lambda declarations are scoped like simple blocks, the keywords `this` and `super` have the same meaning as in the enclosing environment: that is, they refer respectively to the enclosing object and its superclass object. For example, the following program prints the message `Hello, world!` twice to the console:

```
public class Hello {
    Runnable r1 = () -> { System.out.println(this); };
    Runnable r2 = () -> { System.out.println(toString()); };

    public String toString() { return "Hello, world!"; }

    public static void main(String... args) {
        new Hello().r1.run();
        new Hello().r2.run();
    }
}
```

If the same program were written using anonymous inner classes instead of lambdas, it would print the result of calling the `toString` method of `Object` on the inner classes. The more common use case of accessing the current instance of the enclosing object, which is straightforward for lambdas, requires the awkward syntax `OuterClass.this` for anonymous inner classes.

One question often arises in connection with the rule for interpreting `this`: can a lambda refer to itself? A lambda can refer to itself if its name is in scope, but the rules restricting forward references in initializers (for both local and instance variables) prevent lambda variable initialization. It is still possible to declare a recursively defined lambda:

```
public class Factorial {
    IntUnaryOperator fact;
    public Factorial() {
        fact = i -> i == 0 ? 1 : i * fact.applyAsInt(i - 1);
    }
}
```

This idiom is considered adequate for the relatively unusual occasions on which a recursive lambda definition is required.

2.3 Variable Capture

In the previous section, we saw how to interpret names that a lambda expression inherits from its enclosing environment. But name interpretation is only part of the story; once we have understood the meaning of a variable name inherited from the environment, we still have to know what we can do with it—and what we *should* do with it, which may not be the same thing.

First, notice that many useful lambda expressions do not in fact inherit any names from their environment. Object-oriented programmers can understand this by analogy with static methods; although in general the behavior of objects depends on their state, it is often useful to define methods that do not depend on the system state in any way. The utility class `java.lang.Math`, for example, contains only static methods—it makes no sense to take account of the system state in calculating, for example, the square root of a number. Lambdas can fulfill the same role; a lambda that will produce the same result as a call of `Math.sqrt` could be written like this:

```
DoubleUnaryOperator sqrt = x -> Math.sqrt(x)
```

Lambdas like these, which interact with their environment only via arguments and return values, are called *stateless*, or *non-capturing*. *Capturing lambdas*, by contrast, can access the state of their enclosing object. "Capture" is the technical term for the retention by a lambda of a reference to its environment. The connotation is that the variable has been ensnared by the lambda and held, to be queried or—in other languages—modified, when the lambda is later evaluated.

The access provided by capture is restricted; the central principle of the restriction is that captured variables may not have their values changed. So although the traditional term is "variable capture," in fact it would be more accurate to call it "value capture." To understand how the principle is implemented, let's first consider local variable capture; after that, field capture will be a simpler case.

Traditionally, for local classes in general and anonymous inner classes in particular, the only local variables from the enclosing method that could be accessed in the inner class were those declared `final`. The rule for lambdas in Java 8 is very similar, with only a little relaxation of the syntactic requirements: to ensure that a lambda can never change the value of a variable that it has captured from its enclosing environment, the variable must be *effectively final*, meaning that it is never anywhere assigned to after its initialization. (As of Java 8, anonymous and local classes can also access effectively final variables.)

Essentially, effective finality allows omission of the keyword `final` from the declaration of a variable that is going to be treated as final. The restriction of capture to effectively final variables has attracted controversy around the contrast with other languages, for example JavaScript, that do not have this restriction. The justification for preventing mutation of local variables by lambdas is that it would introduce very complex changes that would affect both program correctness and performance, and that it is in any case unnecessary:

- **Correctness**: Lifting this restriction would allow the introduction of a new class of multithreading bugs involving local variables. Local variables in Java have until now been immune to race conditions and visibility problems because they are accessible only to the thread executing the method in which they are declared. But a lambda can be passed from the thread that created it to a different thread, and that immunity would therefore be lost if the lambda, when evaluated by the second thread, were given the ability to mutate local variables.

Further, regardless of the number of threads involved, a lambda can outlive the call to the method that evaluated it. If captured locals were mutable, they too would need to outlive the method call that created them. This change would introduce, among other consequences, a new possibility of memory leaks involving local variables.

- **Performance**: Programs that allow multithread access to mutable variables can be guaranteed correct, if access to the variables is guarded by synchronization. But the cost of this would frustrate one of the principal purposes of introducing lambdas—to allow strategies that efficiently distribute evaluation of a function for different arguments to different threads. Even the ability to read the value of mutable local variables from a different thread would introduce the necessity for synchronization or the use of `volatile` in order to avoid reading stale data.

- **Inessentiality**: Another way to view this restriction is to consider the use cases that it discourages. The idioms that are forbidden by this restriction involve initialization and mutation, like this simple example for summing the values in a `List<Integer>`:

```
int sum = 0;
integerList.forEach(e -> { sum += e; };          // illegal
```

The Stream API offers better alternatives. In this simple case, we can write

```
int sum = integerList.stream()
        .mapToInt(Integer::intValue)
        .sum();
```

A guiding principle of the Java 8 design, explained in detail in the following chapters, is that the effort of learning to use this functional style will be more than repaid by the improvement in code quality that it brings. The fact that code in this style is also *parallel-ready* (§3.1.1) can be seen as a bonus, bringing better performance in some situations now, and in many more situations in future.

It is no secret that the restriction to effective finality is easily evaded. For example, if the local variable is an array reference, the variable can be final but the array contents will still be mutable. You can use this well-known trick to implement an iterative idiom, but then executing in parallel, even unintentionally, will expose race conditions. You can prevent these by synchronization, but only at the cost of increased contention and reduced performance.[3] In short, don't do it!

It appears that no restriction such as effective finality applies to the capture of field names, but this is actually consistent with the treatment of local variables: a reference to a fieldname `foo` is actually a shorthand for `this.foo`, with the pseudo-variable `this` in the role of an effectively immutable local variable. As with a reference to a field of any other object, the only value captured when the lambda is the object reference—in this case, `this`. When the lambda is evaluated, `this` is dereferenced—in the same way as any local reference variable—and the field accessed.

It may appear that the arguments against allowing mutation of local variables should apply to fields as well. But lambdas are intended to provide a gentle impetus away from mutation, where better alternatives are available, not a wholesale conversion of Java into a functional language. The situation prior to Java 8 was that shared variable mutation was easily achieved—perhaps too easily!—and the responsibility on developers was to avoid it or, if that was impossible, to manage it. Mutation of field values by lambdas doesn't change that situation.

2.4 Functional Interfaces

We know from §1.1.3 that a lambda expression must implement a functional interface. But to make practical use of lambdas and functional interfaces, we need to understand the relationship between them more precisely. This section gives an overview and briefly surveys the functional interfaces provided in the library `java.util.function`. Later (in §2.7), we'll explore the relationship in more detail.

The reason that functional interfaces have this central role derives from their most important property, the one that gives them their name: they can be used to describe the type of a function. For example, the interface `UnaryOperator`

```
public interface UnaryOperator<T> { T apply(T t); }
```

describes the function

```
f: T -> T
```

This is its *function type*, which in the simplest and most common case, as here, is just the method type of a functional interface's single abstract method: that is, the method's type parameters, formal parameter types, return types, and—where applicable—thrown types. (Function types were previously called

---

[3] Safer alternatives do exist, like `AtomicInteger` or `LongAdder`. But a still better alternative is to avoid shared variable mutation altogether whenever you can.

"function descriptors"; you may still come across this term.) §2.7.1 explains function types in more detail.

The function type is what a lambda must match, allowing for some adaptation of types through boxing or unboxing, widening or narrowing, etc. For example, suppose we have declared a variable `pointList` as a `List<Point>`, and we now want to replace every element in it. The method `replaceAll` is suitable for this purpose:

List<E>	ⓘ
replaceAll(UnaryOperator<E>)	void

Class Diagram Conventions

The class diagrams for platform library APIs in this book use some simplifying abbreviations:

- The icon at the top right contains "i" or "s" to indicate whether the diagram contains instance or static methods.

- Wildcard bounds on generic parameter types are omitted (for example, the parameter to `forEach` is actually `Consumer<? extends T>`).

- If you see a type variable in a method declaration but not in the class declaration, then you can assume it is a type parameter of the method.

- Diagrams are not necessarily complete—they list only the methods important for the discussion.

The call could look like this:

```
pointList.replaceAll((Point p) -> { /* return new Point object */ });
```

For this to compile, the lambda expression must match the function type of `UnaryOperator<Point>`, which is the type of the method

```
public Point apply(Point p);
```

This case is straightforward, but in general the matching process offers some new challenges to type checking. Previously, any well-formed Java expression had a defined type; now, although every lambda in a well-typed statement or expression implements a functional interface, exactly *which* functional interface it implements is only partly determined by the lambda itself. Enough information must be provided by the context to allow an exact type to be inferred, a process known as *target typing*.[4] Here is an example of a lambda expression that, in isolation, has many possible types:

```
x -> x * 2
```

This expression can be an instance of many functional interfaces, including these two, declared in `java.util.function`:

```
public interface IntUnaryOperator {
    int applyAsInt(int operand);
}
public interface DoubleUnaryOperator {
    double applyAsDouble(double operand);
}
```

So both of the assignments

```
IntUnaryOperator iuo = x -> x * 2;
DoubleUnaryOperator duo = x -> x * 2;
```

are legal, because in each case the type of the lambda expression is compatible with the target type, namely the functional interface type of the variable being assigned. The compiler determines that type for the first case by typing the lambda parameter as `int`, making the lambda as a whole a function from `int` to `int`. That matches the function type of `IntUnaryOperator`, which also takes an `int` and returns an `int`. Similarly, in the second case, the lambda parameter can be typed as `double`, making the lambda a function from `double` to `double`, which matches the function type of `DoubleUnaryOperator`.

Two lambdas can be textually identical, like those we have just seen, but have different types—and different meanings; the operation on `int` values is different from the one on `double`s. The types are established at compile time and cannot be changed, so there is no way of reusing the same lambda text for different types (unless they are compatible by casting in the usual way). The next section shows an example (p. 31).

Table 2-1 shows the four basic types of functional interfaces declared in `java.util.function`, with sample use cases and examples of lambda instances (with the type parameter `T` instantiated to `String` and `U` to `Integer`).

The forty-odd types defined in `java.util.function` are evolved from these four by various combinations of three different routes:

---

[4]Actually, target typing is not altogether new, but its greatly increased use in Java 8 for compiling lambda expressions is a major departure from traditional type checking of Java programs. Until now, the type of an expression has first been computed and then checked for compatibility with its context; if the context is a method call, an appropriate overload is chosen as the context. Untyped lambda expressions, by contrast, have no single type to be checked against the context, so in the case of a method call the overload must be chosen first, but still be compatible with the lambda. This challenge to the compiler is explored further in §§2.7 and 2.8.

Interface	Args.	Returns	Sample Use Case	Example
`Consumer<T>`	`T`	`void`	using objects	`s -> System.out.print(s)`
`Predicate<T>`	`T`	`boolean`	filtering values	`s -> s.isEmpty()`
`Supplier<T>`	`none`	`T`	factory methods	`() -> new String()`
`Function<T,U>`	`T`	`U`	transforming or selecting from objects	`s -> new Integer(s)`

TABLE 2-1.   *Basic functional interfaces in* `java.util.function`

- Primitive specializations: these interfaces replace type parameters with primitive types. Examples include:

  ```
  interface LongFunction<R> { R apply(long value); }
  interface ToIntFunction<T> { int applyAsInt(T value); }
  interface LongToIntFunction { int applyAsInt(long value); }
  ```

- The function types of `Consumer`, `Predicate`, and `Function` all take a single argument. There are corresponding interfaces that take two arguments, for example:

  ```
  interface BiConsumer<T,U> { void accept(T t, U u); }
  interface BiFunction<T,U,R> { R apply(T t,U u); }
  interface ToIntBiFunction<T,U> { int apply(T t, U u); }
  ```

- Common use cases for `Function` require its parameter and result to have the same type. We saw an example of this in the parameter to `List.replaceAll`. These use cases are met by specializing the variations of `Function` to corresponding `Operators`, for example:

  ```
  interface UnaryOperator<T> extends Function<T,T> { ... }
  interface BinaryOperator<T> extends BiFunction<T,T,T> { ... }
  interface IntBinaryOperator { int applyAsInt(int left, int right); }
  ```

This library is a "starter kit," intended to cover the common use cases for functional interfaces. If your use case is not covered, it is easy to declare a functional interface of your own, although it is good practice to make use of those in the library when possible. It is also good practice to annotate custom functional interface declarations with `@FunctionalInterface` so that the compiler can check that your interface declares exactly one abstract method, and so that the Javadoc for it will automatically have an explanatory section added.

2.5 Using Lambda Expressions

A lambda expression can be written wherever a reference to a functional interface instance would be valid, provided that the context of the occurrence provides an appropriate target type—that is, provided the context unambiguously requires a functional interface type. For example, the target type of the declaration

```
IntPredicate ip = i -> i > 0;
```

is `IntPredicate`, a functional interface whose function type is compatible with the lambda `i -> i > 0`. By contrast, the declaration

```
Object o = i -> i > 0;   // invalid
```

does not compile, because the target type required by the context is not that of a functional interface, so does not give the compiler the type information that it needs to compile the lambda.

Six kinds of contexts can provide appropriate target types:

- Method or constructor arguments, for which the target type is the type of the appropriate parameter. We have already seen straightforward examples of this throughout Chapter 1.

- Variable declarations and assignments, for which the target type is the type being assigned to:

```
Comparator<String> cc =
    (String s1, String s2) -> s1.compareToIgnoreCase(s2);
```

Array initializers are similar except that the target type is the type of the array component:

```
IntBinaryOperator[] calculatorOps = new IntBinaryOperator[]{
    (x,y) -> x + y, (x,y) -> x - y, (x,y) -> x * y, (x,y) -> x / y
};
```

Arrays of lambdas have limited application, however, since most functional interfaces are generic, and generic array creation is not allowed.

- Return statements, for which the target type is the return type of the method:

```
Runnable returnDatePrinter() {
    return () -> System.out.print(new Date());
}
```

- Lambda expression bodies, for which the target type is the type expected for the body, which is derived in turn from the outer target type. Consider

```
Callable<Runnable> c = () -> () -> System.out.println("hi");
```

The outer target type here is `Callable<Runnable>`, whose function type is the type of the method

```
Runnable call() throws Exception;
```

so the target type of the lambda body is the function type of `Runnable`, which is the type of the `run` method. This takes no arguments and returns no values, so matches the inner lambda.

- Ternary conditional expressions, for which the target type for both arms is provided by the context. For example:

```
Callable<Integer> c = flag ? (() -> 23) : (() -> 42);
```

- Cast expressions, which provide the target type explicitly. For example:

```
Object o = () -> "hi";            // illegal
Object s = (Supplier) () -> "hi";
Object c = (Callable) () -> "hi";
```

The first of these declarations is illegal because no target type is available to resolve the ambiguous declaration of the lambda. The second and third are legal because the casts provide a target type. This example also illustrates the point that textually identical lambdas can have different types; attempting to reuse a lambda with a different type, for example by writing

```
Callable c1 = (Callable) s;
```

will compile, but would fail at run time with a `ClassCastException`.

2.6 Method and Constructor References

We have seen that any lambda expression may be thought of as an implementation of (in the common case) the single abstract method declaration of a functional interface.

But when a lambda expression is simply a way of calling a named method of an exist-ing class, a better way of writing it may be just using the existing name. For example, consider this code, which prints to the console every element of a list:

```
pointList.forEach(s -> System.out.print(s));
```

The lambda expression here simply passes its argument on to the call of `print`. A lambda like this, whose only purpose is to supply its arguments to a concrete method, is fully defined by the type of that method. So, provided the type can be determined by some means, a shorthand form containing only the method name will provide as much information as the full lambda but in a more readable form. Instead of the preceding code we can write:

```
pointList.forEach(System.out::print);
```

to mean exactly the same thing. This way of writing a handle to a concrete method of an existing class is called a *method reference*. There are four types of method ref-erence, as shown in Table 2-2. The rest of this section explains the purpose of each type.

Name	Syntax	Lambda Equivalent
Static	`RefType::staticMethod`	`(args) -> RefType.staticMethod(args)`
Bound Instance	`expr::instMethod`	`(args) -> expr.instMethod(args)`
Unbound Instance	`RefType::instMethod`	`(arg0,rest) -> arg0.instMethod(rest)`
Constructor	`ClsName::new`	`(args) -> new ClsName(args)`

TABLE 2-2.   *Method Reference Types*

2.6.1 Static Method References

The syntax for static method references simply requires class and static method name, separated by a double colon. For example,

```
String::valueOf
Integer::compare
```

are references to static methods. To see how static method references can be used, suppose we want to sort an array of `Integer` by magnitude, treating the values as unsigned. The natural order for `Integer` is numerical (i.e., it takes account of the sign of values), so we will need to provide an explicit `Comparator`. We can make use of the static method `Integer.compareUnsigned`:

```
(x,y) -> Integer.compareUnsigned(x, y);
```

so sorting our array, `integerArray` say, by this call

```
Arrays.sort(integerArray, (x,y) -> Integer.compareUnsigned(x, y));
```

would be legal, but more verbose and repetitive than its static method reference equivalent:

```
Arrays.sort(integerArray, Integer::compareUnsigned);
```

In fact, this method was introduced in Java 8 partly in anticipation of its use in this way. In the future, one factor in API design will be the desirability of method signatures being suitable for functional interface conversion.

Notice in Table 2-2 that the syntax *ReferenceType::Identifier* doesn't always represent a reference to a static method. As we are about to see, this syntax can be used to reference instance methods as well.

2.6.2 Instance Method References

There are two ways of referring to instance methods. *Bound method references* are analogous to the static case, replacing the form *ReferenceType::Identifier* with *ObjectReference::Identifier*. The example that introduced this section was a bound method reference: the `forEach` method was used to pass each element from a collection into the instance method `print` of the `PrintStream` object `System.out` for processing, replacing the lambda expression

```
pointList.forEach(p -> System.out.print(p));
```

with the bound method reference

```
pointList.forEach(System.out::print);
```

Bound references are so called because the receiver is fixed as part of the method reference. Every invocation of the method reference `System.out::print` will have the same receiver: `System.out`. Often, however, you want to invoke a method reference with the method receiver as well as its arguments taken from the arguments to the method reference. For this, you need an *unbound method reference*, so called because the receiver is not fixed; rather, the first argument to the method reference is used as the receiver. Unbound method references are easiest to understand when there is only one argument; for example, to create a `Comparator` using the factory method `comparing` (p. 16), we could use an unbound reference to replace the lambda expression

```
Comparator personComp = Comparator.comparing(p -> p.getLastName());
```

with the unbound method reference

```
Comparator personComp = Comparator.comparing(Person::getLastName);
```

An unbound method reference can be recognized from its syntax: as with static method references, the form *ReferenceType::Identifier* is used, but in this case *Identifier* refers to an instance method rather than a static one. To explore the difference between bound and unbound method references, consider calling the method `Map.replaceAll` supplying each kind of instance method reference:

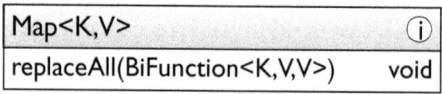

Map<K,V>	ⓘ
replaceAll(BiFunction<K,V,V>)	void

The effect of `Map.replaceAll` is to apply its `BiFunction` argument to every key-value pair in the map, replacing the value component of the key-value pair with the result. So if the variable `map` refers to a `TreeMap` with this as its string representation:

```
{alpha=X, bravo=Y, charlie=Z}
```

then the effect of calling `replaceAll` with a bound method reference

```
String str = "alpha-bravo-charlie";
map.replaceAll(str::replace)
```

would be three applications of `str.replace`, namely:

```
str.replace("alpha","X")
str.replace("bravo","Y")
str.replace("charlie","Z")
```

The result of each call would replace the corresponding value, so afterwards the map would contain

```
{alpha=X-bravo-charlie, bravo=alpha-Y-charlie, charlie=alpha-bravo-Z}
```

Now let's restart the example with `map` at its initial value, and again call `replaceAll`, this time with the unbound method reference `String::concat`, a reference to an instance method of `String` that takes a single argument. It seems strange to be using a one-argument instance method as a `BiFunction`, but in fact it is the method reference that is the `BiFunction`: it is passed two arguments, the key-value pair, and takes the first argument as the receiver, so the method itself is called like this:

```
key.concat(value)
```

The first argument to the method reference is shifted into the receiver position, and the second (and subsequent, if any) arguments are shifted left one position. So the result of the call

```
map.replaceAll(String::concat)
```

is

```
{alpha=alphaX, bravo=bravoY, charlie=charlieZ}
```

2.6.3 Constructor References

In the same way that method references are handles to existing methods, constructor references are handles to existing constructors. Constructor references are created using syntax similar to that of method references, but with the method name replaced by the keyword new. For example:

```
ArrayList::new
File::new
```

As with method references, the choice between overloaded constructors is made using the target type of the context. For example, in the following code, the target type of the map argument is a function of type String -> File; to match this, the File constructor with a single String parameter will be chosen by the compiler.

```
Stream<String> stringStream = Stream.of("a.txt", "b.txt", "c.txt");
Stream<File> fileStream = stringStream.map(File::new);
```

2.7 Type Checking

This section examines the conditions needed for a lambda to match a function type, and the next section explains how type inference can resolve a call to the "best" method overload. These two sections are quite detailed; you may choose either to skip them or scan them quickly on a first reading.

Earlier in this chapter, we saw that a lambda expression can be said to have a single type only when it appears in a context that provides a target type. Expressions like this, whose type is partly decided by their context, are called *poly expressions*. Method and constructor references are also poly expressions; without context, the expression String::valueOf could refer to any of the nine different String methods of that name. This section and the next one explore the process of type checking lambdas and method and constructor references. But since that type checking takes place against a functional interface's function type, it's necessary first to have a precise definition of function types.

2.7.1 What Exactly Is a Function Type?

In the rest of this chapter, the idea of a function type will often be important to understanding how type checking works, so it is worth pinning it down precisely. In fact, the simple definition given in §2.4 is sufficient in most cases: the function type of a functional interface is the type of its single abstract method—that is, its type parameters together with its parameter, return, and thrown types.

However, this simple definition can be complicated by two factors: first, all interfaces declare (implicitly, if not explicitly) abstract methods corresponding to the public methods in `Object`, and the single abstract method of a functional interface is in addition to these. Most often the `Object` methods are declared implicitly, but not always; for example, `Comparator` explicitly declares a method `equals` that matches the `equals` method of `Object`. In such cases the explicit declaration makes no difference; `Comparator` still meets the definition of a functional interface.

The second complicating factor is that two interfaces might have methods that are not identical but are related by erasure. For example, the methods of the two interfaces

```
interface Foo1 { void bar(List<String> arg);}
interface Foo2 { void bar(List arg);}
```

are said to be *override-equivalent*. If the superinterfaces of an interface contain override-equivalent methods, the function type of that interface is the type of a single method that can legally override all the inherited abstract methods. In this example, if

```
interface Foo extends Foo1, Foo2 {}
```

then the function type of `Foo` is the method type corresponding to

```
public void bar(List arg);
```

These complications do not have much general impact on the appealingly simple idea of a single abstract method, but it is useful to bear them in mind when encountering corner cases like `Comparator`.

2.7.2 Matching a Function Type

Type checking a lambda against a functional interface type provided by target typing requires that the lambda expression be *compatible* with the interface's function type. For example, the assignment

```
UnaryOperator<Integer> b = x -> x.intValue();
```

compiles because the lambda expression is compatible with the function type of `UnaryOperator<Integer>`. These are the conditions for compatibility to hold:[5]

Arities   The lambda and the function type must have the same number of arguments.

Parameter types   If the lambda expression is explicitly typed, the types must exactly match the parameters of the function type; if the lambda is implicitly typed then, for return type checking (in the next step), its argument types are assumed to be the same as those of the function type.

Return types

- If the function type returns `void`, then the lambda body must be a statement expression (i.e., an expression that can be used as a statement, like a method call or an assignment), for example:

  ```
  (int i) -> i++;
  ```

  —notice that the value of the statement expression is discarded—or a block body without a value-bearing[6] return statement, for example:

  ```
  (Thread t) -> { t.start(); }
  ```

- If the function type has a non-`void` return type, then the lambda body must return an assignment-compatible value. For example, this lambda body returns an `int` value, to be assigned to the `Integer` result of the `UnaryOperator`'s function type:

  ```
  UnaryOperator<Integer> b = x -> x.intValue();
  ```

To the compatibility conditions just given, a further condition must be added to ensure that a lambda expression will compile:

Thrown types   A lambda can throw a checked exception only if that exception, or one of its supertypes, is declared to be thrown by the function type.

This last condition can cause problems. For example, suppose we want to declare a method to centralize the handling of `IOException` for a number of different I/O operations implemented by parameterless methods of `File`. A first thought might be to declare it like this:

---

[5] This section is a simplified version of §15.27.3 of the Java 8 Edition of *The Java Language Specification* (http://docs.oracle.com/javase/specs/jls/se8/html/).

[6] The use of "value-bearing" or "stream-bearing" to describe methods that return values or streams will soon become common enough to use without explanation; not quite yet, however.

```
<U> U executeFileOp(File f, Function<File,U> fileOp) { ... }
```

but the function type for `Function` does not declare any exceptions, so a call like

```
executeFileOp(f, File::delete);
```

will fail to compile. Instead, a custom functional interface is needed:

```
@FunctionalInterface
interface IOFunction<T,R> {
    R apply(T t) throws IOException;
}
```

so that we can then declare `executeFileOp` as we intended:

```
<U> U executeFileOp(File f, IOFunction<File,U> fileOp) {
    try {
        return fileOp.apply(f);
    } catch (IOException e) {
        // centralized exception handling
    }
}
```

To summarize: a lambda can handle an exception thrown to it in the same two possible ways as any other method—it can (implicitly) declare it to its caller or it can handle it in a `catch` block. Since none of the library functional interfaces declare any exceptions, a lambda can only pass an exception to its caller if it implements a user-defined functional interface, as in the example. By contrast, we will see in §5.3 that for stream processing we have to take the alternative route of handling checked exceptions inside lambdas, since the parameters of the stream processing operations are all library functional interfaces. To summarize more briefly: checked exception handling is a problem area in the design of Java 8 lambdas.

2.8 Overload Resolution

Using the compatibility criteria of §2.7.2, target typing of lambda expressions is straightforward when the functional interface type can be determined without ambiguity. Most of the target type contexts listed in §2.5 provide unambiguous contexts. Unfortunately, the most commonly used contexts for lambda expressions—method call sites—can also be the most problematic when the method in question has different overloaded variants. The difficulties described in this section are not commonly met; when they do appear, however, they can lead to frustrating compilation problems. And if you are designing an API, your users are depending on you to avoid them. So it is worth studying the topic now—forewarned is forearmed!

Here is a short summary of the challenge of overload resolution: calls to overloads of different arities are usually easily distinguished, but choosing between two overloads of the same arity requires the compiler to know the type of the arguments being supplied. In the case of an untyped lambda this is a problem, since its type cannot be inferred without a target type, and the target type is provided by the method declaration, so cannot be known until overload resolution is done! It's possible to break this circularity by imposing some arbitrary rules, making the process of type inference counterintuitive and unpredictable, or to force the user to supply lambda parameter types. To avoid these undesirable alternatives, the designers ended up making overload resolution more tolerant of reasoning under uncertainty and designing new APIs so as to allow effective overload resolution with implicitly typed lambdas.

2.8.1 Overloading with Lambda Expressions

Before exploring the difficulties of using type inference, let's see how it works in a straightforward case. Chapter 1 (§1.4) introduced the method `Comparator` `.comparing` which, given a key extractor, creates a `Comparator` from it. This is one overload of `comparing` (with most type bounds omitted for readability):

```
public static <T,U extends Comparable<U>>
        Comparator<T> comparing(Function<T,U> keyExtractor)
```
❶

Suppose that we want to sort strings by their length. Given an unambiguous target type such as assignment provides, `comparing` can take an untyped lambda and use it to create a comparator for the purpose:

```
Comparator<String> cs = Comparator.comparing(s -> s.length());
```
❷

Here is a highly simplified account of how the lambda type in ❷ is resolved. First, the compiler must choose a set of `comparing` overloads against which to check the lambda. This set can only contain ❶, given that the other overload has two arguments. Now that the overload has been chosen, matching the return type of ❶ against the target type provided by ❷ allows the compiler to deduce that in this case `T` is `String`. Now the lambda expression can be matched against the function type for `Function<T,U>`:

```
public U apply(T t)
```

Since the argument type `T` to the lambda is known to be `String`, the type returned by `String.length`—which is `int`, boxed to `Integer`—can be substituted for `U`. All the types are now known and the type bound on `U` in ❶, which guarantees that the result of the lambda implements `Comparable`, can be checked for `Integer`. Everything is consistent, and the call can be compiled.

So far, so good. But suppose that `Comparator` declared another overload of `comparing`:

```
// removed from the JDK
public static <T>
        Comparator<T> comparing(ToIntFunction<T> keyExtractor)        ❸
```

At one time in the development of Java 8, this overload really did exist. If we try again to type check ❷ in its presence, we will see why it was withdrawn. Following the same process as before, the compiler first tries to choose a set of overloads to type check. The rule is that this must be done *before* any type checking of untyped lambdas. (Certain untyped lambdas could in fact be type checked before method overload resolution, but this was abandoned when the designers found that it made the overall process more inconsistent and confusing.)

Given that rule, there is little information available to help with method overload resolution. The compiler cannot use the target type provided by the assignment context, because another important rule says that a method call with a given set of arguments must be resolved to the same overload anywhere it occurs, regardless of context. It can use other arguments to the method call, but in this case there are none. It can use some information from the lambda expression, but for the compatibility conditions an untyped lambda like this one can only report the number of arguments it accepts and whether it is returning a value. In this case, those are no help either: the lambda accepts one argument and returns a value, matching the function types of both candidate functional interfaces. So progress is blocked and the compiler reports an error, with the message "reference to comparing is ambiguous."

How could we avoid this? If the lambda's argument type were known, the compiler could use that information to check both of the candidate function types, using the algorithm described at the start of this section. Since the argument type is `String`, it would find them both compatible with the lambda. It could then choose between them on the basis of which returns the most specific result: `ToIntFunction` returns an `int`, which matches more closely against the return type of `String.length` than does `Integer`, as returned by `Function<String,Integer>`. So the call

```
Comparator<String> cs = Comparator.comparing((String s) -> s.length());
```

would compile, resolving to ❸. For `Comparator.comparing`, the Java 8 designers wanted to avoid forcing the user to provide explicit lambda typing in this way, so they replaced the overloads that accepted `ToIntFunction`, `ToLongFunction`, and `ToDoubleFunction` with new methods `comparingInt`, `comparingLong`, and `comparingDouble`. For other APIs, it may be possible to provide different overloads with functional interface parameters with different arities, or to provide other disambiguating parameters to the overload. If you are designing an API, your users will thank you for choosing one of these alternatives.

2.8.2 Overloading with Method References

Method and constructor references add another difficulty: if the method or constructor they refer to is generic or overloaded, they are called *inexact*, because their syntax allows no equivalent to explicit lambda typing, so you cannot specify the precise type at which you intend them to be used. Note that this is a relatively unusual situation: in practice, most methods are neither overloaded nor generic. As we see at the end of this section, difficulties with inexact method references can be avoided by using typed lambdas instead, and it can be argued that this should be your first, rather than your last, resort.

For an example of an inexact constructor reference, `Exception::new` could refer to either of the constructors for `Exception`, including these two:

```
public Exception()
public Exception(String message)
```

The first of these could match the function type of `Supplier<Exception>`, and the second could match the function type of `Function<String,Exception>`. So if we declare method overloads

```
<T> void foo(Supplier<T> factory)
<T,U> void foo(Function<T,U> transformer)
```

then a call to

```
foo(Exception::new);
```

will fail to compile with the error message "reference to foo is ambiguous." However, although we can't make the constructor reference exact as we could by explicitly typing a lambda, there is a remedy: since `foo` is generic, we can specify which type instantiation we want for it by providing a *type witness*. This syntax requires the receiver to be stated explicitly:

```
this.<Exception>foo(Exception::new);
this.<String,Exception>foo(Exception::new);
```

Of course, this will only work to distinguish generic methods with different numbers of type arguments. Suppose instead that we want to call one of two method overloads:

```
void bar(IntFunction<String> f)
void bar(DoubleFunction<String> f)
```

with a reference to `String.valueOf`, a static method with overloads that match both `IntFunction<String>` and `DoubleFunction<String>`. Here, only a cast can save the situation:

```
bar((IntFunction<String>) String::valueOf);
bar((DoubleFunction<String>) String::valueOf);
```

This problem only arises because `String::valueOf` is overloaded in such a way that its different function types match the possible types of the single parameter that distinguishes the different overloads of `bar`. Although this situation can occur in real life, it will probably not be common. If it does occur, remember that you can always use the lambda equivalent:

```
bar((double i) -> String.valueOf(i));
bar((int i) -> String.valueOf(i));
```

To summarize: if type inference or overload resolution fails, you need to supply more type information. Of the different ways of doing this, the least intrusive is to find an equivalent typed lambda or exact method reference. Failing that, supply a type witness. In terms of code style, casting is a last resort; avoid it if you can.

2.9 Conclusion

We've now seen all of the syntax changes needed to introduce lambdas; the other major change for Java 8, the introduction of default methods, supports API evolution by allowing interfaces to define behavior. Default methods will be covered in Chapter 7. Some of the details in this chapter may have seemed intricate, but overall, the ideas are quite simple, much simpler in fact than seemed achievable at many points in the long debate that led to their final form.

Language evolution is always hard because of the number of interactions that each new feature can have with existing ones; a case in point is the complexity, outlined in this chapter, that boxing/unboxing and untyped poly expressions have brought to method overload resolution. Another is the difficulty of writing lambdas that throw checked exceptions. Of the many trade-offs that had to be considered in the design and implementation of lambda syntax, the ones involving type inference will probably be most noticeable, in particular because it sometimes seems less powerful than you would expect. That is because the overriding motivation in designing the type inference rules was to make them simple and consistent—the same motivation that guided the entire language design.

CHAPTER
3

Introduction to Streams
and Pipelines

I n Chapter 1 we saw two main themes in the motivations for introducing lambdas to Java. These two themes—better code and easier parallelism—come together in the introduction of streams for processing collections. Although lambda expressions are (in practice) essential for programming with streams, they are not enough: to use streams effectively, we need some new ideas specific to the programming model that they enable. In this chapter, we'll explore the basic ideas underlying streams, with relatively straightforward examples of stream operations that should help to develop a basic intuition about how they work. In later chapters, we will go further, exploring some more theoretical topics, seeing how stream code can simplify common collection processing tasks, and finally investigating the performance of sequential and parallel streams in different situations.

The individual stream operations that we will learn about may not seem very powerful on their own. The power of the Stream API lies in the possibilities that are created by composing these operations together. In this, its design draws on long historical precedent in computing. One of its closest antecedents is the so-called "Unix philosophy," of which the authors of *The Unix Programming Environment* (Kernighan and Pike, 1984) wrote

> *At its heart is the idea that the power of a system comes more from the relationships among programs than from the programs themselves. Many UNIX programs do quite trivial things in isolation, but, combined with other programs, become general and useful tools.*

If you are familiar with the realization of that philosophy in the Unix pipeline, you will see that reflected clearly in the intermediate operations of streams. But, more broadly, the principle of composability was central throughout the design of the Java 8 changes: in §1.4 we saw how lambda expressions enable the design of finer-grained, more composable operations, and later we will see its influence in the design of stream collectors.

In following the trail that takes us through the technical detail of streams, we should be sure not to lose sight of their fundamental justification: the more expressive formulation of common aggregate operations. The success of the stream mechanism will be assessed by how far it achieves the goal of clearer expression of common business logic.

3.1 Stream Fundamentals

Streams were introduced in §1.2 as optionally ordered *value sequences*. In operational terms, they differ from collections in that they do not store values; their purpose is to process them. For example, consider a stream having a collection as its source: creating it causes no data to flow; when values are required by the terminal operation, the stream provides them by pulling them from the collection; finally, when all the collection values have been provided by the stream, it is *exhausted* and cannot be used any further. But this is not the same as being empty; streams never hold values at any point. Streams with non-collection sources behave very similarly: for example, we could generate and print the first ten powers of two by means of the following code:

```
IntStream.iterate(1, i -> i*2)
    .limit(10)
    .forEachOrdered(System.out::println);
```

Although, as we will see later, the method `iterate` generates an infinite stream, the function represented by the lambda is called only as often—in this case, nine times—as a value is required for downstream processing.

The central idea behind streams is *lazy evaluation*: no value is ever computed until it is required. Java programmers already know about laziness:[1] iterators, which we use every day—explicitly or implicitly—have this characteristic. Creation of an iterator doesn't cause any value processing to take place; only a call to its `next` method makes it actually return values from its collection. Streams are conceptually quite similar to iterators, but with important improvements:

- They handle exhaustion in a more client-friendly way. Iterators can signal exhaustion only by returning `false` from a `hasNext` call, so clients must test for it each time they require an element. This interaction is inherently fault-prone, because the time gap between the call of `hasNext` and `next` is a window of opportunity for thread interference. Moreover, it forces element processing into a sequential straitjacket, implemented by a complex and often inefficient interaction between client and library.

- Unlike iterators, which always yield their values in a deterministic sequence, streams can be *unordered*. We'll explore this in detail in Chapter 6; for the moment, all you need to know is that opportunities for optimizing a parallel stream arise when we are unconcerned about the order in which its values are presented.

- They have methods (the intermediate operations) that accept behavioral parameters—transformations on streams—and return the stream resulting from the transformation. This allows streams to be chained together into pipelines, as we saw in Chapter 1, providing not only a fluent style of programming, but also the opportunity of big performance gains. We'll study intermediate operations in detail later in this chapter.

---

[1] All programmers should know about laziness, of course, since it is the first of the three great virtues of a programmer: Laziness, Impatience, and Hubris (Larry Wall et al., *Programming Perl*, O'Reilly, 2012.)

- They retain information about the properties of their source—for example, whether the source values are ordered, or whether their count is known—that allows optimizations of value processing in ways not possible with iterators, which retain no information besides the values themselves.

One big advantage of lazy evaluation can be seen in the "search" methods of Stream: findFirst, findAny, anyMatch, allMatch, and noneMatch. These are called "short-circuit" operators because they often make it unnecessary to process all the elements of a stream. For example, anyMatch has to find only a single stream element that satisfies its predicate (boolean-valued function) for stream processing to be complete, just as allMatch has only to find one that fails to satisfy its predicate. The ability to avoid generating and processing unnecessary elements can obviously save a great deal of work—and, in the case of infinite streams, it is only the combination of lazy evaluation and short-circuit operators that makes it possible to complete stream processing at all. True, this advantage of lazy evaluation can also, in principle, be realized by iterators (in the case of collections processing) or explicit looping (in the case of generator functions), but code using the Stream API is much easier to read and (eventually) to write.

Lazy evaluation provides another major advantage: it allows multiple logical operations to be fused together into a single pass on the data. Recall the code developed in Chapter 1 to first illustrate the idea of a pipeline:

```
OptionalDouble maxDistance =
    intList.parallelStream()
        .map(i -> new Point(i % 3, i / 3))
        .mapToDouble(p -> p.distance(0, 0))
        .max();
```

The fluent style is natural and easy to read, but to understand what is happening you need to bear in mind the implication of lazy evaluation. It is easier to see this if, for demonstration purposes, the pipeline is broken into a stream declaration and the terminal operation call:

```
DoubleStream ds =
    intList.parallelStream()
        .map(i -> new Point(i % 3, i / 3))
        .mapToDouble(p -> p.distance(0, 0));

// the pipeline has now been set up, but no data has been processed yet

OptionalDouble maxDistance = ds.max();
```

Separating out the terminal operation call clarifies the situation: it is directly calling the transformational code of the behavioral parameters, which is all executed in a single pass. Moreover, because for each element these operations are executed by a single thread, optimizations that depend on code and data locality can operate.

This is a very different model from bulk collection processing, which is normally implemented by a series of passes, each one transforming every element of a collection and storing the results in a new one. In Chapter 1 we saw how a sequence of loops (e.g., p. 10) can be translated into an equivalent sequence of stream operations (p. 12). The stream code is both pithier and more efficient (as reported on p. 148), because it is implemented by fusing the separate loop operations.

3.1.1 Parallel-Ready Code

Lazy value sequences are a very old idea in programming; what distinguishes their implementation in Java is the extension of this concept to include parallel processing of their elements. Although sequential processing is still a very important model for computing, it is no longer the unique reference model: as Chapter 1 explained, parallel processing has become so important that we have to rethink our model of computation towards one that results in code that is agnostic about how it is executed, whether sequentially or in parallel. In that way, both our code—and even more importantly, our coding style—is insured against the need to change when, in the future, the balance of advantage tilts towards parallel execution. The Stream API encourages this view; a key to understanding it is the insight that all operations are defined to have equivalent effect in sequential and in parallel modes, provided that the programmer follows some simple rules. In fact, this way of thinking about processing modes could be deduced from the choice of the single `Stream` interface to represent both sequential and parallel streams; the API designers explored the idea of providing sequential-only and parallel-only methods in separate interfaces, and rejected it.

Notice that this definitely does not mean operations will always produce exactly the same result in each mode: `forEach`, for example, is explicitly allowed to execute in nondeterministic order. In sequential mode it may preserve ordering, by happy accident of the implementation, but it is a mistake to depend on this; `forEach` and other nondeterministic operations are *equally* nondeterministic in sequential and in parallel mode. Conversely, an operation that is defined to be deterministic in either mode is guaranteed to work deterministically in both. The motivation for providing nondeterministic operations like `forEach` is provided by situations where unnecessary determinism has a significant performance cost.[2] Choosing a deterministic alternative, like `forEachOrdered`, requires a conscious judgement that ordering is a requirement of the problem, rather than just an accidental by-product of the implementation.

---

[2] A well-known example of this is the `ReentrantLock` class, which can be created with either a fair (deterministic) or non-fair (nondeterministic) thread scheduling policy. Fair locks are at least an order of magnitude less efficient and in practice are rarely used, as fair scheduling is not often required (Brian Goetz et al., *Java Concurrency in Practice*, Addison-Wesley, 2006.)

This insight also helps to explain the choice of operations defined in the API, which avoids any that could not be implemented equally well in sequential and parallel modes. Some "obvious" operations conceal a deep sequential bias—for example, the "takeWhile" operation, which on other platforms processes a stream until it encounters a sentinel value. While this operation is not actually infeasible in parallel, its implementation would have been so expensive—both in design and execution—that it was deprioritized.

This change in thinking can be reframed: programs with iteration contain two different kinds of information: what is to be done, and how it is to be done. Decoupling these two kinds of content leads to a development model in which we write *parallel-ready* code specifying functional behavior alone, and then separately specify its execution mode—ideally, delegating the implementation of the execution to a library. This is a big change: for many of us, the sequential model is so deeply ingrained that it will take an effort to adjust to the implications of dethroning it. But that effort will be worthwhile; not only will the resulting programs be future-proof, but our code will be clearer, more concise, and more maintainable.

3.1.2 Primitive Streams

The introduction of auto-boxing and -unboxing in Java 5 gave programmers some license to ignore the difference between values of a primitive type and those of the corresponding wrapper type. The compiler can often detect that a primitive value is being supplied in a method call or assignment in place of a wrapper value (or vice versa) and will insert the appropriate conversion. This is convenient and often gives rise to more readable programs; generic collection classes can now appear to contain primitive values, and wrapper types fit much better than do primitives with Java's basic object-oriented programming model. But it can lead to repeated boxing and unboxing operations, with high performance costs. For example, incrementing the variable i in the innocent-looking code

```
Optional<Integer> max = Arrays.asList(1,2,3,4,5).stream()
    .map(i -> i + 1)
    .max(Integer::compareTo);
```

involves executing the Integer methods intValue and valueOf, respectively, before and after every addition. We would like to avoid such overheads in applications that process large collections of values; one way of doing this is to define streams whose elements are already primitive rather than reference values. This decision brings advantages besides improved performance, in the form of useful numeric-only methods like sum and the ability to create streams containing ranges of numbers. For example, using the type IntStream, representing a stream of primitive int values, the preceding code can be rewritten:

```
OptionalInt max = IntStream.rangeClosed(1,5)
    .map(i -> i + 1)
    .max();
```

The improvements here are both in readability, with specialized `range` and `max` methods, and in efficiency, with no requirement for boxing and unboxing. §6.6 reports the performance difference between these two code fragments, for various range sizes. For sufficiently large data sets, the unboxed code is an order of magnitude faster.

The primitive stream types are `IntStream`, `LongStream`, and `DoubleStream`— chosen as the most commonly used numeric types, the ones for which the cost-benefit trade-off was most favorable. In case your application requires streams of one of the other numeric types, these are also supported: `float` values can be embedded in a `DoubleStream`, and `char`, `short`, and `byte` values in an `IntStream`. The APIs of the primitive streams are very similar to one another, and all are sufficiently similar to the reference stream type `Stream` to be discussed together in this chapter. As a preliminary, it is worth noting the possible stream type interconversions:

- The primitive stream types `IntStream` and `LongStream` have methods `asDoubleStream` and (for `IntStream`) `asLongStream`, which apply the appropriate widening coercion to each primitive value, for example:

  ```
  DoubleStream ds = IntStream.rangeClosed(1, 10).asDoubleStream();
  ```

- For boxing, each of the primitive stream types has a method `boxed`, which returns a `Stream` of the appropriate wrapper type, for example:

  ```
  Stream<Integer> is = IntStream.rangeClosed(1, 10).boxed();
  ```

- For unboxing, a `Stream` of wrapper values can be converted to a primitive stream by calling the appropriate map conversion operations (which we will see in more detail later in this section), supplying the appropriate unboxing method. For example, the following code creates a `Stream<Integer>`, then converts it to an `IntStream`:

  ```
  Stream<Integer> integerStream = Stream.of(1, 2);
  IntStream intStream = integerStream.mapToInt(Integer::intValue);
  ```

3.2 Anatomy of a Pipeline

The full power of streams is realized by the pipelines we create by composing them together. We have seen examples of the various stages of a pipeline: its origin in a stream source, its successive transformations through intermediate operations, and its ending in a terminal operation. In the remainder of this chapter we will look at each of these stages closely enough to build an intuition for the possibilities of stream programming; subsequent chapters will explore the features that give them their full power.

3.2.1 Starting Pipelines

Up to this point, the data for our stream processing examples have been drawn from collections. In fact, since the advantages of the stream processing model apply to all kinds of bulk data, many classes in the platform library that can produce bulk data can now also create streams supplying that data. However, in this chapter we are mainly concerned with gaining an intuition of how streams work, so the complete list of stream-creating methods in the platform library is delayed to Chapter 5. For now, all that we need are the stream-bearing methods of `Collection` and the factory methods in the stream interfaces:

- `java.util.Collection<T>`: The default methods on this interface will probably be the most commonly used ways of generating streams:[3]

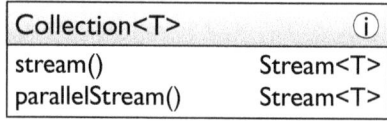

Collection<T>	ⓘ
stream()	Stream<T>
parallelStream()	Stream<T>

   The contract for `parallelStream` actually states that its return is a "possibly parallel `Stream`." As we will see, it is the collection's responsibility to present its data in parallel, and not every collection can achieve that. Although this will affect performance, it has no impact on functional behavior. We will explore this issue fully in Chapter 6.

- `java.util.stream.Stream<T>`: This interface exposes a number of static factory methods, with default implementations. In this chapter, we shall be using `Stream.empty` and two overloads of `Stream.of` (the primitive stream types have analogous methods):

---

[3] The conventions for API diagrams are listed in the box on page 27. In brief: the icon at top right indicates whether the diagram contains static or instance methods; wildcard bounds on generic types are omitted; undeclared generic types in method signatures can be assumed to be method type parameters; diagrams show only selected methods of the class or interface.

Stream<T>	Ⓢ
empty()	Stream<T>
of(T)	Stream<T>
of(T...)	Stream<T>

These methods are enough to start our exploration of the features of streams and pipelines; in Chapter 5 we will investigate other stream-bearing methods of the platform libraries.

3.2.2 Transforming Pipelines

Following stream creation, the next stage of a pipeline consists of a number (possibly zero) of intermediate operations. As we have seen, intermediate operations are lazy: they only compute values as required by the eager operation that terminates the pipeline.

This and the following two chapters explore the Stream API with examples of its use on a tiny example domain. I've just moved to an apartment with enough bookshelf space to allow me to organize my collection of a few hundred books haphazardly acquired over the last several decades. The system I'm planning will model this library as a `Collection` of `Book` objects:

Book	ⓘ
getTitle()	String
getAuthors()	List<String>
getPageCounts()	int[ ]
getTopic()	Topic
getPubDate()	Year
getHeight()	double

To understand the examples, the properties need some explanation:

- `Topic` is an `enum`, with members HISTORY, PROGRAMMING, and so on.

- The property `pageCounts` refers to the page counts of the volumes that comprise multi-volume titles. It has been given an array type, not to recommend the use of arrays—for most purposes, Java arrays should be regarded as a legacy type, to be replaced by `List` implementations where possible—but because arrays of primitive types are still often encountered in maintaining legacy code, and we need to become familiar with the stream idioms for processing them.

- Multiple editions of a book, all with the same title and authors, can coexist in the library if they have different publication dates.

- The physical height of a book is important to me; my built-in bookshelves have different heights, so I will need to take book heights into account when I'm deciding where to shelve the different topics.

In exploring the different stream operations, it will be useful to have a few concrete examples to focus on. Here are declarations for three books from my library:

```
Book nails = new Book("Fundamentals of Chinese Fingernail Image",
    Arrays.asList("Li", "Fu", "Li"),
    new int[]{256},       // pageCount per volume
    Year.of(2014),        // publication date
    25.2,                 // height in cms
    MEDICINE);

Book dragon = new Book("Compilers: Principles, Techniques and Tools",
    Arrays.asList("Aho", "Lam", "Sethi", "Ullman"),
    new int[]{1009},
    Year.of(2006),        // publication date (2nd edition)
    23.6,
    COMPUTING);

Book voss = new Book("Voss",
    Arrays.asList("Patrick White"),
    new int[]{478},
    Year.of(1957),
    19.8,
    FICTION);

Book lotr = new Book("Lord of the Rings",
    Arrays.asList("Tolkien"),
    new int[]{531, 416, 624},
    Year.of(1955),
    23.0,
    FICTION);
```

In the examples that follow, a real-life persistence mechanism has been replaced by a placeholder variable `library`, declared as a `List<Book>`. Figure 3-1 presents examples of code using streams to process my library; they are all explained later in this chapter, but are collected together here to give you an idea of what is possible using stream processing.

This section will explore the action of the various intermediate operations by looking at examples of how each could be used in operations to process my library. Although it will mainly discuss operations on the reference stream type `Stream`, the

---

Examples of Stream Processing

A stream that contains only computing books:

```
Stream<Book> computingBooks = library.stream()
    .filter(b -> b.getTopic() == COMPUTING);
```

A stream of book titles:

```
Stream <String> bookTitles = library.stream()
    .map(Book::getTitle);
```

A stream of Book, sorted by title:

```
Stream<Book> booksSortedByTitle = library.stream()
    .sorted(Comparator.comparing(Book::getTitle));
```

Use this sorted stream to create a stream of authors, in order of book title, with duplicates removed:

```
Stream<String> authorsInBookTitleOrder = library.stream()
    .sorted(Comparator.comparing(Book::getTitle))
    .flatMap(book -> book.getAuthors().stream())
    .distinct();
```

A stream yielding the first 100 books in alphabetical order of title:

```
Stream<Book> readingList = library.stream()
    .sorted(Comparator.comparing(Book::getTitle))
    .limit(100);
```

A stream with the rest:

```
Stream<Book> remainderList = library.stream()
    .sorted(Comparator.comparing(Book::getTitle))
    .skip(100);
```

The earliest-published book in my library:

```
Optional<Book> oldest = library.stream()
    .min(Comparator.comparing(Book::getPubDate));
```

The set of titles of the books in my library:

```
Set<String> titles = library.stream()
    .map(Book::getTitle)
    .collect(Collectors.toSet());
```

FIGURE 3-1. *Examples of* Stream *operations from this chapter*

ideas carry over to primitive stream types also; for intermediate operations, their API closely resembles that of `Stream`.

Filtering

The method `filter` allows selective processing of stream elements:

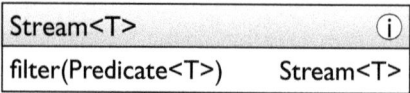

Stream<T>	ⓘ
filter(Predicate<T>)	Stream<T>

Its output is a stream containing only those elements of the input stream that satisfy the supplied `Predicate` (p. 29). For example, we could isolate the computing books in my collection by constructing this stream:

```
Stream<Book> computingBooks = library.stream()
    .filter(b -> b.getTopic() == COMPUTING);
```

Figure 3-2 illustrates the action of `filter`. In part (a) two `Book` elements are arriving on the input stream: `nails`, followed by `dragon`; in part (b) the output stream contains only `dragon`, as that is the only one whose topic is COMPUTING.

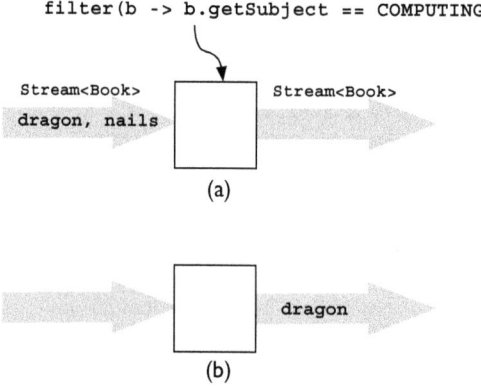

FIGURE 3-2.   *How* `Stream.filter` *works*

Mapping

The method `map` transforms each stream element individually using the supplied `Function<T,R>` (p. 29):

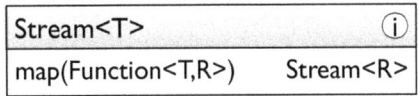

Its output is a stream containing the results of applying the `Function` to each element of the input stream. For example, it could be used to create a `Stream` of publication dates:

```
Stream<Year> bookTitles = library.stream()
    .map(Book::getPubDate);
```

Figure 3-3 illustrates the action of `map`. In part (a) the input elements are the same two `Book` instances; in part (b) the resulting stream contains references to the `Year` objects obtained by calling `getPubDate` on each instance.

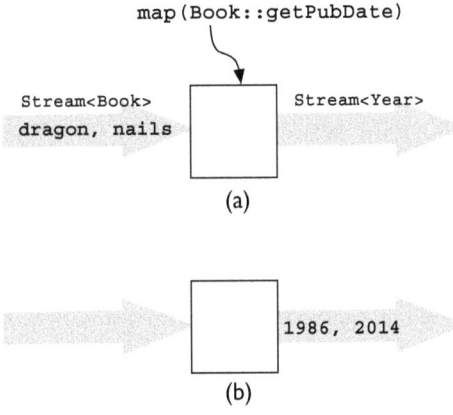

FIGURE 3-3. *How* `Stream.map` *works*

The methods `mapToInt`, `mapToLong`, and `mapToDouble` correspond to `map`. They convert reference type streams to primitive streams using instances of `ToIntFunction<T>`, `ToLongFunction<T>`, or `ToDoubleFunction<T>`, each of which take a `T` and return a primitive value:

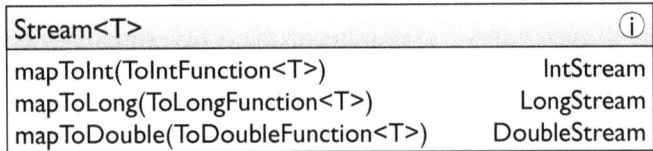

On p. 49 we saw that these methods can be used to unbox a stream of wrapper values. For another example, I could count the total number of authorships (defining an authorship as the contribution of an author to a book) of all books in my library like this:

```
int totalAuthorships = library.stream()
    .mapToInt(b -> b.getAuthors().size())
    .sum();
```

Converting to primitive streams in this way allows us to take advantage of their better performance and of their specialized arithmetic terminal operations, like `sum`.

The Stream API supports interconversion between each of the four `Stream` types. So, besides the `Stream` methods discussed here, each of the primitive streams has three conversion `map` operations, one for each of the three other types. For example, `IntStream` has, besides `map`, conversion operations `mapToLong`, `mapToDouble`, and `mapToObj`.

One-to-Many Mapping

An alternative (though less efficient) way of implementing the last example would be to convert the stream of `Book` into a stream of `Author`, each one representing an authorship. We could then simply apply the terminal operation `count` to find the number of elements in the stream. But `map` isn't suitable for this purpose, because it performs a one-to-one transformation on elements of the input stream whereas this problem requires a single `Book` to be transformed to several `Author` elements in the output stream. The operation we need will map each `Book` into a stream of `Author`—writing, say, `book.getAuthors().stream()`—then flatten the resulting series of streams into a single stream of `Author` for all books. That is the operation `flatMap`:

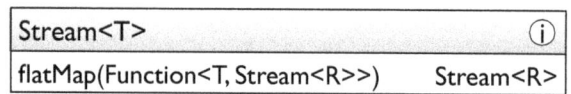

Stream<T>	ⓘ
flatMap(Function<T, Stream<R>>)	Stream<R>

For this example we would write:

```
Stream<String> authorStream = library.stream()
    .flatMap(b -> b.getAuthors().stream());
```

Figure 3-4 shows how it works. In part (a) the same two `Book` instances are on the input stream, in (b) each is mapped to a stream of `String`, and in (c) these individual streams are fed into the output stream.

Like the methods corresponding to `map` for conversion to primitive streams, there are primitive conversion methods: `flatMapToInt`, `flatMapToLong`, and `flatMapToDouble`. For example, we could get the total page count of all volumes

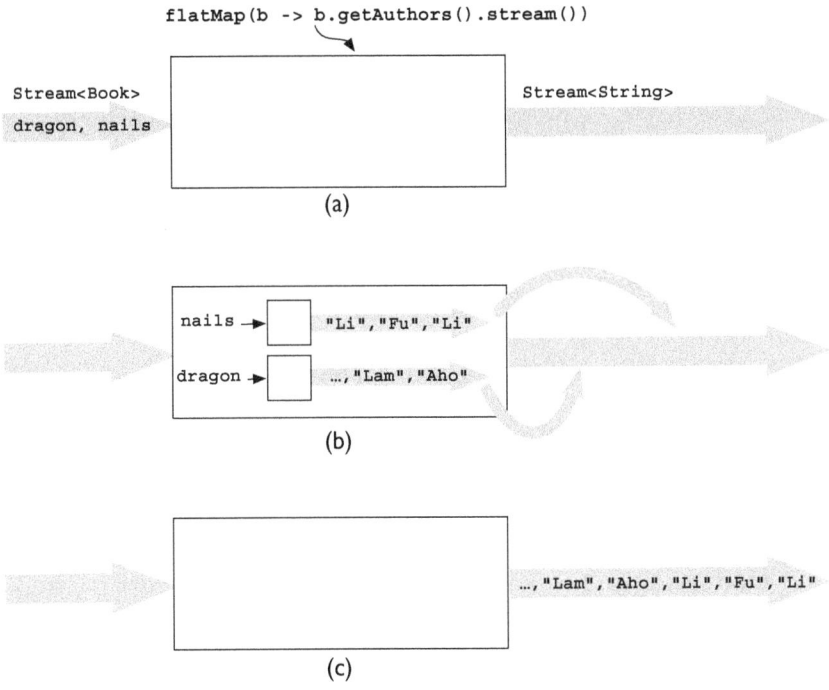

FIGURE 3-4. *How* `Stream.flatMap` *works*

of all books by creating an individual `IntStream` for each `Book` using `IntStream.of` and then concatenating them using `flatMapToInt`:

```
int totalPageCount = library.stream()
    .flatMapToInt(b -> IntStream.of(b.getPageCounts()))
    .sum();
```

The primitive stream types have only `flatMap`; there are no type conversion flat-mapping operations.

Debugging

As we saw in §3.1, calling the terminal operation of a pipeline results in the execution of a fusion of its intermediate operations. As a result, the usual debugging technique of stepping through operations is not available for streams. The alternative provided by the Stream API, the operation `peek`, differs from other intermediate operations in that the output stream contains the same elements, and in the same order, as the input stream. The purpose of `peek` is to allow processing to be carried out on elements of streams that are intermediate in a pipeline; for example, we could print the title of every book that passes a filter before sending them downstream for further processing (in this case, accumulating them to a `List`: see §3.2.4):

```
List<Book> multipleAuthoredHistories = library.stream()
    .filter(b -> b.getTopic() == Book.Topic.HISTORY)
    .peek(b -> System.out.println(b.getTitle()))
    .filter(b -> b.getAuthors().size() > 1)
    .collect(toList());
```

If you are familiar with Unix pipelines, you will recognize the similarity to `tee`, though `peek` is more general, accepting any appropriately typed `Consumer` as its argument. This method was provided to support debugging and, because it works by means of side-effects, should not be used for any other purpose. The issues of side-effects and interference are explored in §3.2.3.

Sorting and Deduplicating

The operation `sorted` behaves as we would expect: the output stream contains the elements of the input stream in sorted order.

Stream<T>	ⓘ
sorted()	Stream<T>
sorted(Comparator<T>)	Stream<T>
distinct()	Stream<T>

The sorting algorithm is stable on streams having an encounter order (see Chapter 6); this means that when ordered streams are sorted, the relative order of elements with equal keys will be maintained between the input and the output.

The first `sorted` overload sorts objects using their natural order (footnote, p. 15). For example, we might use it to create a stream of `Book` titles, sorted alphabetically:

```
Stream<String> sortedTitles = library.stream()
    .map(Book::getTitle)
    .sorted();
```

The second overload accepts a `Comparator`; for example, the static method `Comparator.comparing` (p. 16) creates a `Comparator` from a key extractor:

```
Stream<Book> booksSortedByTitle = library.stream()
    .sorted(Comparator.comparing(Book::getTitle));
```

This provides an alternative to natural ordering on the stream elements by creating a `Comparator` from a key. Notice that here also you are not confined to natural ordering: another overload of `Comparator.comparing` accepts a `Comparator` on the extracted keys, allowing you to impose a different ordering on them. For example, to sort my books by the number of authors, I could write

```
Stream<Book> booksSortedByAuthorCount = library.stream()
    .sorted(Comparator.comparing(Book::getAuthors,
                        Comparator.comparing(List::size)));
```

The second operation in this group, `distinct`, removes duplicates from a stream. Its output is a stream containing only a single occurrence of each of the elements in its input—all duplicates, according to the `equals` method, are dropped. For example, to use the sorted stream of books we just created to produce a list of authors, but with duplicates removed, we would write

```
Stream<String> authorsInBookTitleOrder = library.stream()
    .sorted(Comparator.comparing(Book::getTitle))
    .flatMap(book -> book.getAuthors().stream())
    .distinct();
```

Since the `equals` method may not take account of all the fields of a stream element, "duplicates" may in fact be distinguishable by other methods. So the idea of stability, discussed in connection with `sorted`, also applies to `distinct`: if the input stream is ordered, the relative order of elements is maintained. From a number of equal elements, the first will be chosen; if the input stream is unordered, any element may be chosen (likely to be a less expensive operation in parallel pipelines).

Truncating

This category groups two operations that constrain the output from streams:

Stream<T>	ⓘ
skip(long)	Stream<T>
limit(long)	Stream<T>

The operations `skip` and `limit` are duals: `skip` discards the first *n* stream elements, returning a stream with the remainder, whereas `limit` preserves the first *n* elements, returning a stream containing only those elements. For example, we could get the first 100 books in alphabetical order of title by writing:

```
Stream<Book> readingList = library.stream()
    .sorted(Comparator.comparing(Book::getTitle))
    .limit(100);
```

Of course, there may be fewer than 100 books in the library; in that case, the stream that `limit` returns will contain all of them. Analogously, `skip` could be used to create a stream containing all but the first 100 elements:

```
Stream<Book> remainderList = library.stream()
    .sorted(Comparator.comparing(Book::getTitle))
    .skip(100);
```

3.2.3 Non-interference

Among the features that the Stream API offers programmers is the execution of parallel operations—even on non-threadsafe data structures. This is a valuable benefit, so it should not be surprising that it does not come entirely free of charge. The cost is cooperation with the programming model, according to the rules described in this section. These are not arbitrary restrictions; indeed, they restrict you only if you are thinking in sequential mode. If you are already designing parallel-ready code, they will seem natural because your thinking will be free of hidden assumptions about which thread will execute the behavioral parameters to stream operations, and about the order in which elements will be processed. You will be aware that, potentially, every behavioral parameter can be executed in a different thread, and that the only ordering constraint is imposed by the encounter order (§6.4) of the stream.

The rules are mostly to protect your program from interference between the multiple threads required for parallel execution. Sometimes the framework itself provides that guarantee, as we will see that it does for collectors. But it makes no such guarantee for the behavioral parameters to stream operations. Here is an example of how *not* to create a classification map, mapping each topic to a list of books on that topic:

```
// behavioral parameter with state - don't do this!
Map<Topic,List<Book>> booksByTopic = new HashMap<>();
library.parallelStream()
    .peek(b -> {
        Topic topic = b.getTopic();
        List<Book> currentBooksForTopic = booksByTopic.get(topic);
        if (currentBooksForTopic == null) {
            currentBooksForTopic = new ArrayList<>();
        }
        currentBooksForTopic.add(b);
    booksByTopic.put(topic, currentBooksForTopic);  // don't do this!
    })
    .anyMatch(b -> false);  // throw the stream elements away
```

The lambda that forms the behavioral parameter to `peek` is not threadsafe. When it is executed in parallel, only bad things can happen: map entries will be lost (up to 1 percent of them on my modestly parallel Core 2 Duo machine); very possibly, the call of `currentBooksForTopic.add` will throw an `ArrayIndexOutOfBoundsException`. To correct this problem in the wrong way, the body of the lambda would have to be synchronized, leading to a clumsy and inefficient solution. To correct it in the right way requires attention to the principle that *behavioral parameters should be stateless*. The Stream API is designed to provide safe and performant parallel-friendly alternatives to code like this—in this case, the `groupingBy` collectors, which we will meet in the next section.

It's tempting to think that such problems needn't concern you if you never use parallel streams in your own code, just as a previous generation of programmers mistakenly thought that problems of synchronization needn't concern them if they weren't using threads. As library APIs make increasing use of streams in the future, you will find yourself calling methods accepting `Stream` parameters. If you create a pipeline with non-threadsafe behavioral parameters like the one we just saw:

```
Stream<Book> books = library.stream()
    .peek(/* non-threadsafe behavioral parameter */);
```

and then call a library method supplying `books` as an argument, the library method may well call `parallel` on your stream before calling a terminal operation, resulting in the same race conditions as before. The method `parallel`, like `sequential`, provides a hint to the implementation about which execution mode to choose; the execution mode is fixed for the entire pipeline only at the point that terminal operation execution begins, so control over it does not remain with you as the creator of the pipeline. The lesson of this example is once again that a stream with a non-threadsafe behavioral parameter is an accident waiting to happen.

The classification map example of this section might lead you to think that the main problem with stateful behavioral parameters is thread safety. In fact, the documentation of `java.util.stream` gives a general description of a stateful operation as "one whose result depends on any state that might change during the execution of the stream pipeline." For an example of a stateful operation that goes wrong despite being threadsafe, let's allow each `Book` to refer to another and to contain a `boolean` field indicating whether it is referred to. For a test, we could set up a `List<Book>`, each referring to an adjacent element in the list (treating the list as circular), then execute this code:

```
long count = bookList().stream()
    .peek(b -> b.refersTo.referred = true)
    .filter(b -> b.referred)     // stateful!
    .count();
```

If I run this sequentially on a list of 1000 elements, I get either 1 or 999 as a result, depending on whether each element refers to its predecessor or successor. (This difference, which is entirely dependent on the implementation's choice of evaluation order, is sufficient reason in itself to avoid code like this.) But running it in parallel gives inconsistent results varying unpredictably between 1 and 4 or else 995 and 999.

An equally important requirement on parallel-ready code is that pipelines must *avoid mutating their source* during the execution of their terminal operation. Considering only collections for a moment, that prohibition may remind you of the rule that disallows structural alterations during iteration: a "fail-fast" iterator—one created by a non-threadsafe collection—throws `ConcurrentModificationException` if it detects structural changes to its collection (other than those that it has itself made). Spliterators (§5.2), the parallel analog of iterators, behave similarly if they detect structural changes to a stream source during terminal operation execution.

This is the most likely symptom of concurrent stream source modification, but by no means the only one: `ConcurrentModificationException` is thrown only by *structural* modifications—typically, addition or removal of a collection element. But the rules for streams forbid *any* modification of stream sources—including, for example, changing the value of an element—by any thread, not only pipeline operations. (The only exceptions to this rule are threadsafe concurrent data structures, like those in `java.util.concurrent`.) This is actually a rather modest restriction, considering what it makes possible: the ability to perform parallel operations on non-threadsafe data structures.

3.2.4 Ending Pipelines

The examples of the previous section have one thing in common: because the stream operations that they illustrate are all lazy, their effect is to combine individual streams into pipelines without initiating any element processing. By contrast, the operations in this section are all eager; calling any of them on a stream starts the evaluation of the stream elements, pulling the elements through the stream from its source. Since all of them produce non-stream results, they could all be said in some sense to reduce the stream contents to a single value. But it is useful to further divide them into three categories:

- Search operations, which are used to detect a stream element satisfying some constraint, so may sometimes complete without processing the entire stream.

- Reductions, which return a single value that in some way summarizes the values of the stream elements. This topic is big enough to require the next chapter all to itself. For now, we will restrict our view to two aspects: convenience reduction methods like `count` and `max`, and simple *collectors*, which terminate streams by accumulating their elements in a collection.

- Side-effecting operations, a category that contains only two methods: `forEach` and `forEachOrdered`. These are the only terminal operations in the Stream API that are designed to be used with side-effects.

Search Operations

The `Stream` methods that can be classified as "search" operations fall into two groups: the first group comprises matching operations, which test whether any or all stream elements satisfy a given `Predicate`:

Stream<T>	ⓘ
anyMatch(Predicate<T>)	boolean
allMatch(Predicate<T>)	boolean
noneMatch(Predicate<T>)	boolean

The names are indicative: `anyMatch` returns `true` on finding an element that satisfies the predicate; `allMatch` returns `false` on finding any element that does not satisfy it, and returns `true` otherwise; `noneMatch` is analogous, returning `false` on finding any element that does satisfy it, and returning `true` otherwise.

For example, planning the organization of my bookshelves is complicated by the fact that these built-in shelves are not all of the same height. If I need to know whether my history books can be placed on the top shelf, whose headroom is only 19 cm, I can write:

```
boolean withinShelfHeight = library.stream()
    .filter(b -> b.getTopic() == HISTORY)
    .allMatch(b -> b.getHeight() < 19);
```

But this is not really what I want if I am planning the allocation of topics to shelves. It would be much better to determine in a single operation all of the topics that would fit on this low shelf (or, better still, to calculate for each topic what headroom it requires). This aim can be achieved by wrapping this code in a loop, but only at the cost of repeatedly calling `library.stream`—an inefficient and ugly solution. In Chapter 4 we will see much better solutions using collectors.

Note that, in accordance with the standard rules of logic, `allMatch` called on an empty stream will always return `true`.

The second group of search operations is made up of the two "find" methods: `findFirst` and `findAny`:

Stream<T>	ⓘ
findFirst()	Optional<T>
findAny()	Optional<T>

These return a stream element if any is available, possibly differing in which one they return. The return type needs a little explanation. At first sight, we might naïvely expect to write

```
Book anyBook = library.stream()
    .filter(b -> b.getAuthors().contains("Herman Melville"))
    .findAny();  // doesn't compile
```

But what if `library` contains no elements, so the stream that it sources is empty? In this situation, there is no answer for `findAny` to return. The traditional Java solution of returning `null` is unsatisfactory: it is ambiguous as to whether a `null` was actually matched in the stream or whether it indicates the absence of a value, as in the result of `Map.get`. Moreover, `null` cannot be used with primitive streams. The alternative created in Java 8 is the class `java.util.Optional<T>`; an instance of this class is a wrapper that may or may not contain a non-null value of type `T`. The "find" methods allow for the possibility of an empty stream by returning `Optional`, so the correct version of the preceding code is

```
Optional<Book> anyBook = library.stream()
    .filter(b -> b.getAuthors().contains("Herman Melville"))
    .findAny();
```

The next section provides a brief overview of the `Optional` class.

By contrast to `findAny`, and provided the stream is ordered, `findFirst` will return the first element that it encounters. For example, we could find the first line in the text of this book containing the string "findFirst":

```
BufferedReader br = new BufferedReader(new FileReader("Mastering.tex"));
Optional<String> line = br.lines()
    .filter(s -> s.contains("findFirst"))
    .findFirst();
```

The use case for `findFirst` is situations like this, where the problem statement concerns finding the first match in an ordered stream. If any match in an ordered stream is acceptable, on the other hand, you should prefer `findAny`; `findFirst` would be liable to do unnecessary work in maintaining an order that is not needed. With an unordered stream, there is no real distinction between the two methods.

The search operations combine with lazy evaluation to save work, as described at the beginning of this chapter: the matching methods can return after finding a single element that satisfies (or not, depending on the particular matching operation) its `Predicate`. The "find" methods always return on finding a single element. Lazy evaluation ensures that when, in these cases, stream processing stops, no (or few) unnecessary elements have been generated.

The class `Optional`

In the last section we saw `Optional<T>` used as a return value from `find` operations, and earlier (§3.1.2) we encountered one of its primitive variants `OptionalInt`. We need `Optional` and its variants when applying terminal operations to empty streams—for example, one for which a filter has eliminated all its elements. The last section described the problems of using `null`; `Optional<T>` avoids these by providing a special empty value that can never be confused with a `T`.

For the limited use we will make of `Optional` in this book, it is enough to briefly explain a few of the methods that allow client code to use its value:

Optional<T>	ⓘ
get()	T
ifPresent(Consumer<T>)	void
isPresent()	boolean
orElse(T)	T
orElseGet(Supplier<T>)	T

The purpose of these operations is as follows:

- `get`: Returns a value if one is present; otherwise, this method throws `NoSuchElementException`. This is the "unsafe" operation for accessing an `Optional`'s contents, normally to be avoided in favor of one of the following safe alternatives.

- `ifPresent`: If a value is present, supplies it to the `Consumer`; otherwise, does nothing.

- `isPresent`: Returns `true` if a value is present; otherwise, returns `false`.

- `orElse`: Returns the value if present; otherwise, returns the argument. This and `orElseGet` are the safe operations for accessing the contents. In the normal use of `Optional`, with the possibility of an empty value, these operations are more useful than `get`.

- `orElseGet`: Returns the value if present; otherwise, invokes the `Supplier` and returns its result.

Reduction Methods

The Stream API is designed, to borrow Larry Wall's well-known slogan, to make the easy jobs easy without making the hard jobs impossible. We shall see how to do the hard jobs, using collectors and spliterators, in the next two chapters. But in practice, most jobs are easy ones, and for these we have convenience reductions—specialized variants of `Stream.reduce` (§4.4), designed for simplicity of use. Here the numeric primitive streams, for example `IntStream`, provide more features:

IntStream	ⓘ
sum()	int
min()	OptionalInt
max()	OptionalInt
count()	long
average()	OptionalDouble
summaryStatistics()	IntSummaryStatistics

These methods are self-explanatory except for the last, `summaryStatistics`. This creates an instance of the class `IntSummaryStatistics`, a value object with five properties: `average`, `count`, `max`, `min`, and `sum`. It is useful in situations in which we want multiple results from a single pass over the data. For example, code to obtain and print the summary statistics of the page count of the books in my library (summing the page count for works spanning multiple volumes) like this:

```
IntSummaryStatistics pageCountStatistics = library.stream()
    .mapToInt(b -> IntStream.of(b.getPageCounts()).sum())
    .summaryStatistics();
System.out.println(pageCountStatistics);
```

produces this output:

```
IntSummaryStatistics{count=409, sum=93641, min=158, average=228.9511,↵
                                                         max=1472}
```

The same pattern appears in `LongStream` and `DoubleStream`. Reference streams also have some convenience reduction methods:

Stream<T>	ⓘ
count()	long
min(Comparator<T>)	Optional<T>
max(Comparator<T>)	Optional<T>

For example, this code will find the earliest-published book in my library:

```
Optional<Book> oldest = library.stream()
    .min(Comparator.comparing(Book::getPubDate));
```

Notice that to find the minimum or maximum of `Stream` elements that have a natural order, you have to provide an explicit `Comparator`. For example, to find the first book title in my library, in alphabetical order, I could write:

```
Optional<String> firstTitle = library.stream()
    .map(Book::getTitle)
    .min(Comparator.naturalOrder());
```

An analogous factory class `Comparator.reverseOrder` is provided for reverse natural ordering.

Collecting Stream Elements

The second kind of reduction, for reference streams, uses `Stream.collect` to accumulate stream values in mutable containers like the classes of the Java Collections Framework. This is called *mutable reduction*:

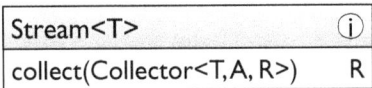

Stream<T>	ⓘ
collect(Collector<T, A, R>)	R

The argument to `collect` is an instance of the `Collector` interface. As the figure shows, `Collector` has three type parameters: the first is the type being collected, and the third is the type of the result container; the second one will be explained in §4.3.1, as part of a more detailed exploration of collectors.

Most collection use cases are covered by predefined `Collector` implementations returned by factory methods of the class `Collectors`. This chapter covers three of the simplest of these methods; in Chapter 4 we will see the full range, and—if you need something beyond what the predefined implementations provide—how you can write your own.

The three factory methods covered here collect to an implementation, chosen by the framework, of one of the three main Java Collections Framework interfaces: `Set`, `List`, and `Map`. Here are the declarations of the methods `toSet` and `toList`.

Collectors	Ⓢ
toSet()	Collector<T, ?, Set<T>>
toList()	Collector<T, ?, List<T>>

For example, to collect the titles of the books in my library into a `Set`, I can write:

```
Set<String> titles = library.stream()
    .map(Book::getTitle)
    .collect(Collectors.toSet());
```

The usual idiom is to statically import the `Collectors` factory methods, making the last line of this example

```
    .collect(toSet());
```

Figure 3-5 shows how this collector works for these two books. In part (a) the input elements are the two `Book` instances we saw earlier. In (b) they are being placed in the `Set`; internally, that operation is implemented using the method `Set.add`, with the usual semantics: elements are unordered and duplicates discarded. In (c) the stream is exhausted and the populated container is being returned from the collector.

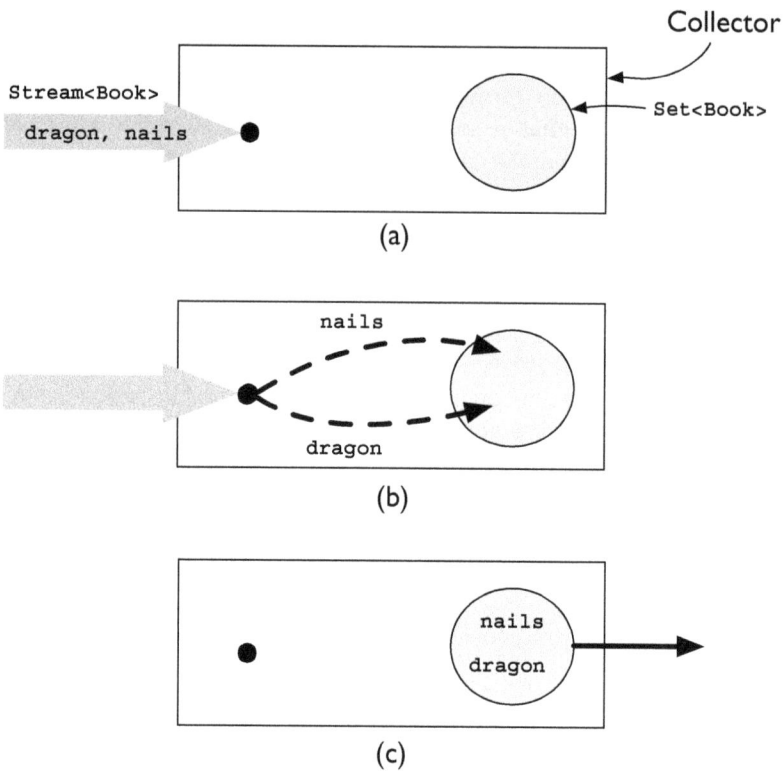

FIGURE 3-5. *How Collectors.toSet works*

The method `toList` is closely analogous to `toSet`, with the method `List.add` implementing the accumulation; so, if the stream is ordered, the created `List` has the same ordering. (If not, stream elements are added in nondeterministic order.) Creating a collector that accumulates to a `Map`, however, is a little more complex. Two method overloads of `toMap` are provided for this, each accepting a key-extracting function from `T` to `K` and a value-extracting function from `T` to `U`. Both of these functions are applied to each stream element to produce a key-value pair.

Collectors	ⓢ
toMap(Function<T,K>, Function<T,U>)	Collector<T, ?, Map<K,U>>
toMap(Function<T,K>, Function<T,U>, BinaryOperator<U>)	Collector<T, ?, Map<K,U>>

For example, I could use a collector from the first overload of `toMap` to map each book title in my collection to its publication date:

```
Map<String,Year> titleToPubDate = library.stream()
    .collect(toMap(Book::getTitle, Book::getPubDate));
```

Figure 3-6 shows how the two functions provided to the `toMap` collector work to populate the `Map`.

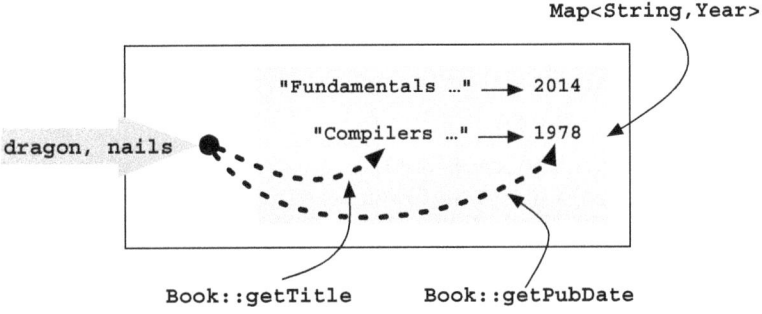

FIGURE 3-6.   *How* `Collectors.toMap` *works*

The second overload of `toMap` is provided to take account of duplicate keys. If I am enthusiastic about a book, I may buy a copy of each new edition as it is published. Different editions have the same title but different publication dates. Of course a `Map` cannot contain duplicate keys, so with the code above a book in multiple editions will cause the collector to throw `IllegalStateException`. That overload, then, is the one to choose when duplicate keys are not expected.

When duplicate keys are expected, the second overload allows the programmer to specify what should happen, in the form of a *merge function*, of type `BinaryOperator<U>`, that produces a new value from the two existing ones—the one already in the map, and the one that is to be added. There are various ways in which two values could be used to produce a third one of the same type; two `String` values could be concatenated, for example. Here I might decide to include only the latest edition of each book in the mapping:

```
Map<String,Year> titleToPubDate = library.stream()
    .collect(toMap(Book::getTitle,
                 Book::getPubDate,
                 (x, y) -> x.isAfter(y) ? x : y));
```

Because the collectors returned by `toMap`—like those returned by `toSet` and `toList`—are accumulating into non-threadsafe containers, managing the accumulation of results from multiple threads is an overhead that can hurt performance on parallel streams. We will see options for collecting more efficiently to `Maps` in Chapter 4, and in Chapter 6 we will explore the impact of collectors on stream performance.

Side-Effecting Operations

We first met these operations at the beginning of this book, as the simplest way of replacing external iteration. They terminate a stream, applying the same `Consumer` to each element in turn. They are the main exception to the convention that the Stream API does not support operations with side-effects:

Stream<T>	ⓘ
forEach(Consumer<T>)	void
forEachOrdered(Consumer<T>)	void

We have seen both of these methods in use already. The main difference between them is obvious from the names: `forEach` is designed for efficient execution on parallel streams, so it does not preserve encounter order. Less obviously, it makes no guarantee about the synchronization of its operations, which can be executed on different threads. So, for example, suppose I wanted to calculate the total page count of all the books in my library, and naïvely declared an instance variable `pageCount` to calculate the total by writing, I might then write:

```
// don't do this - race conditions!
library.stream()
    .forEach(b -> {pageCount += b.getPageCount();});
```

This code is incorrect because the additions to `pageCount` can occur in different threads without synchronization, so is subject to a race condition (simultaneous interfering execution). Of course, the principle of writing parallel-ready code should have warned me against this code even though the stream is sequential. As reinforcement, the API documentation for `forEach` warns me that the action will be executed "in whatever thread the library chooses."

That code could be "corrected" by using `forEachOrdered`, which preserves ordering and guarantees synchronization, instead of `forEach`. Then I could rely on the result from this code:

```
// formally correct but inefficient and ugly
library.stream()
    .forEachOrdered(b -> {pageCount += b.getPageCount();});
```

but although this code works, it is not parallel-ready; the use of `forEachOrdered` forces execution into a sequential mode. Code written in the spirit of the Stream API is both much more readable and more efficient in the general case:

```
int totalPageCount = library.stream()
    .mapToInt(Book::getPageCount)
    .sum();
```

3.3 Conclusion

We now have an overview of the basic operation of streams and pipelines, but we have yet to see many practical examples of using this style of programming to solve real processing problems. In the next two chapters we will build on what we have learned, exploring the API in more detail and investigating strategies for breaking down complex queries into step-by-step operations on streams.

CHAPTER
4

Ending Streams:
Collection and Reduction

P ipelines are ended by terminal operations, which we saw in Chapter 3 are divided into three groups: search operations, reductions, and operations with side-effects. Although we surveyed all three groups then, there is much more to say about reductions; this chapter takes up that story.

Broadly speaking, reductions are operations which return a single value that in some way summarizes the values of the stream elements. But this description does not make a distinction—very important to Java programmers—between summarizing operations that create new objects and those that change their operands. Traditional ideas about reduction have been developed for languages supporting immutability; although modern Java programming practice encourages immutability in general, most pipelines will end in mutable collections. So *collection*, also called *mutable reduction*, is the most important kind of terminal operation in the Stream API. Collection is a generalization of classical reduction, which in Java programming will be useful mainly with primitive streams. Collection is like reduction in the sense that it summarizes values of stream elements into a single object, but it does so via mutation.

Here is a very simple comparison between traditional Java bulk processing code and collection. If we allow a real-life data source to be modeled by an `Iterable<Book>`, declared here as `library`, we would usually accumulate values from it to a `List<Book>` like this:

```
List<Book> bookList = new ArrayList<>();
for (Book b : library ) {
    bookList.add(b);
}
```

In Java 8, now modelling the data source by a `Stream<Book>`, we could get a similar effect by writing

```
List<Book> bookList = libraryStream
    .collect(Collectors.toList());
```

The collector version has a number of advantages, beyond the obvious improvement in conciseness and readability: the stream operations can be safely executed in parallel, even if the `List` into which the stream elements are accumulated (`ArrayList` is used in the current implementation) is not threadsafe. Further, the collector pattern turns out to be very flexible, and collectors are easily composed: Figure 4-1 provides a preview of examples developed later in this chapter to give an advance idea of this flexibility.

In the imperative version, the key components are the creation of the container (`new ArrayList<>()`) and the accumulation of elements into it (`bookList.add(b)`). Collectors also have components for these two tasks, called, respectively, the *supplier* and the *accumulator*. We can identify these components on the diagrams introduced

---

Examples of the Collector Pattern

A map classifying books by topic:

```
Map<Topic,List<Book>> booksByTopic = library.stream()
    .collect(groupingBy(Book::getTopic));
```

An ordered map from book titles to publication date of latest edition:

```
Map<String,Year> titleToPubDate = library.stream()
    .collect(toMap(Book::getTitle,
                   Book::getPubDate,
                   BinaryOperator.maxBy(naturalOrder()),
                   TreeMap::new));
```

A map partitioning books into fiction (mapped to `true`) and non-fiction (`false`):

```
Map<Boolean,List<Book>> fictionOrNon = library.stream()
    .collect(partitioningBy(b -> b.getTopic() == FICTION));
```

A map associating each topic with the book on that topic having the most authors:

```
Map<Topic,Optional<Book>> mostAuthorsByTopic = library.stream()
    .collect(groupingBy(Book::getTopic,
        maxBy(comparing(b -> b.getAuthors().size()))));
```

A map associating each topic with the total number of volumes on that topic:

```
Map<Topic,Integer> volumeCountByTopic = library.stream()
    .collect(groupingBy(Book::getTopic,
        summingInt(b -> b.getPageCounts().length)));
```

The topic with the most books:

```
Optional<Topic> mostPopularTopic = library.stream()
    .collect(groupingBy(Book::getTopic, counting()))
    .entrySet().stream()
    .max(Map.Entry.comparingByValue())
    .map(Map.Entry::getKey);
```

A map from each topic to the concatenation of all the book titles on that topic:

```
Map<Topic,String> concatenatedTitlesByTopic = library.stream()
    .collect(groupingBy(Book::getTopic,
        mapping(Book::getTitle, joining(";"))));
```

FIGURE 4-1. *Examples of* `Stream` *operations from this chapter*

in Chapter 3. Figure 4-2 shows the relationship between Figure 3-5 (p. 68), the diagram for the collector created by `Collectors.toSet`, and these two components.

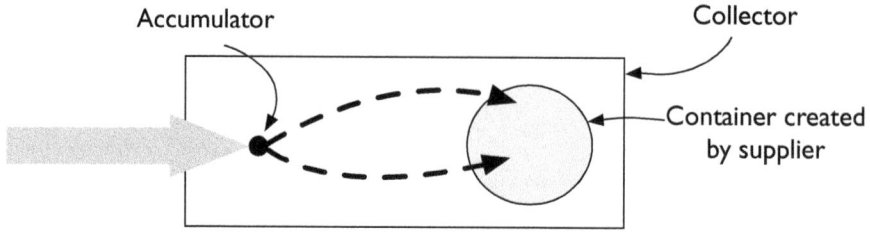

Accumulator   Collector

Container created by supplier

FIGURE 4-2. *The components of* `Collector.toSet`

The supplier defines the container type, always shown shaded in these diagrams (in Figure 4-2, a framework-chosen implementation of `Set<Book>`). The accumulator populates the container from the incoming stream; in Figure 4-2, it is `Set::add`.

4.1 Using Collectors

Later sections of this chapter explore the idea of the collector pattern in depth, and discuss when and how you might want to create a custom collector. But before that, we should consider the most common and straightforward occurrence of the pattern in everyday programming: namely, the use of predefined collectors supplied by the factory methods of the `Collectors` class. These can be divided into two types: stand-alone collectors, useful in their own right, and collectors designed for use in composition with others.

4.1.1 Stand-alone Predefined Collectors

Stand-alone collectors can be divided into three groups, depending on their function:

- To accumulate to framework-supplied containers.
- To accumulate to custom collections.
- To accumulate elements into a *classification map*.

We already met most of the first group in Chapter 3 (p. 67ff)—those for which the supplier is the constructor for a framework-supplied collection: for `toSet` it is an implementation of `Set`, for `toList` of `List`, and for the two overloads of `toMap` it is an implementation of `Map`. The accumulators for these collectors are also obvious: for the `Collection` implementations it is `add`, and for the `toMap` collectors, `put`.

The remaining method in this group is `joining`, which returns a collector that concatenates a stream of `String` objects into a `StringBuilder` whose contents are then returned as a `String` (this is further explained in §4.3.1):

Collectors	Ⓢ
joining()	Collector<CharSequence,?,String>
joining(CharSequence)	Collector<CharSequence,?,String>
joining(CharSequence, CharSequence, CharSequence)	Collector<CharSequence,?,String>

The first overload of `joining` simply concatenates the strings in its input stream. The second overload accepts a `CharSequence`, inserting it as a delimiter between its input strings. For example, here is code to concatenate the titles of all books in my library, separating the titles by a double colon:

```
String concatenatedTitles = library.stream()
    .map(Book::getTitle)
    .collect(joining("::"));
```

The third overload accepts a delimiter, a prefix, and a suffix: for example, for a book `b`, the following code will produce a string concatenating the book's authors, separated by commas, beginning with the book's title and ending with a newline:

```
b.getAuthors().stream().collect(joining(
        ",",
        b.getTitle() +": ",
        "\\n"))
```

We could use this code to create a list of strings, each containing all the authors' names for a single book:

```
List<String> authorsForBooks = library.stream()
    .map(b -> b.getAuthors().stream()
        .collect(joining(", ", b.getTitle() + ": ", "")))
        .collect(toList());
```

The collectors we have seen so far all accumulate to a collection chosen by the framework. Many `Collectors` methods have variants that let you specify a supplier for the container:

Collectors	Ⓢ

`<M extends Map<K,U>>`	`toMap(Function<T,K> keyExtracter,`
	`Function<T,U> valueExtracter,`
	`BinaryOperator<U> mergeFunction,`
	`Supplier<M> mapFactory`
	`)`
	<div align="right">`Collector<T,?,M>`</div>

`<C extends Collection<T>>`	`toCollection(Supplier<C> collectionFactory`
	`)`
	<div align="right">`Collector<T,?,C>`</div>

For example, on page 69 we saw `toMap` used with a merge function to construct a map from book titles to the date of the latest edition. If the contents of the map will subsequently be required in alphabetical order of titles, placing them into a sorted map might improve performance:

```
Map<String,Year> titleToPubDate = library.stream()
    .collect(toMap(Book::getTitle,
                Book::getPubDate,
                (x, y) -> x.isAfter(y) ? x : y,           ❶
                TreeMap::new));
```

Since the merge function is actually choosing the greater of two values of `java.time.Year` using its natural order, line ❶ can be replaced by

```
BinaryOperator.maxBy(Comparator.naturalOrder());
```

The three overloads of `toMap` that we have now seen are increasingly general: the first one we met would accept only key- and value-extracting functions. The second accepts in addition a merge function, and this third one also accepts a supplier. This means that if you want to specify a supplier, you must also provide a merge function. But if you want to, you can re-create the behavior of the simple overload of `toMap` in the presence of duplicate keys by supplying

```
(x,y) -> { throw new IllegalStateException(); }
```

as the third argument to this overload.

You might expect that corresponding overloads of `toList` and `toSet` would be provided to create collectors capable of allowing the specification of custom suppliers. In fact, rather than providing both `toList` and `toSet` with an extra overload, a single more general method `toCollection` has been provided instead. This is more versatile: it allows us to choose not only arbitrary implementations of `Set` and `List`, but of any subinterface of `Collection`. For example, we can collect stream elements into a sorted set or into a blocking queue:

```
NavigableSet<String> sortedTitles = library.stream()
    .map(Book::getTitle)
    .collect(toCollection(TreeSet::new));

BlockingQueue<Book> queueInPubDateOrder = library.stream()
    .sorted(Comparator.comparing(Book::getPubDate))
    .collect(toCollection(LinkedBlockingQueue::new));
```

A third group of `Collectors` methods return collectors with the function of *classifying* stream elements. They are related to the collectors returned by `toMap`, with the difference that instead of using a value-extracting function, the values they place in the map are the elements themselves—or rather, lists of the elements, one `List` corresponding to each classification key:

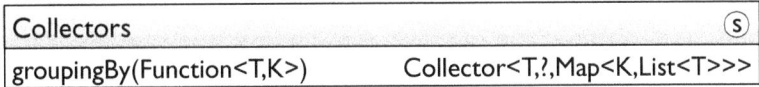

Collectors	ⓢ
groupingBy(Function<T,K>)	Collector<T,?,Map<K,List<T>>>

For example, I could classify my books by topic as follows:

```
Map<Topic,List<Book>> booksByTopic = library.stream()
    .collect(groupingBy(Book::getTopic));
```

Figure 4-3 shows how this example works: for each incoming element, the classifier function is called to determine the key. If the key is not present, it is added, with the value being a singleton `List` containing only the current element. If the key and a `List` value are already present, the stream element is added to the list. The supplier for this collector is the no-arguments constructor for a framework-chosen implementation of `Map<Topic,List<Book>>`, and the accumulator has the function of adding each incoming element as just described. Both of these defaults can be overridden, as we shall see in the next section.

A variant of `groupingBy` is the convenience method `partitioningBy`, in which the key type `K` is specialized to `Boolean`:

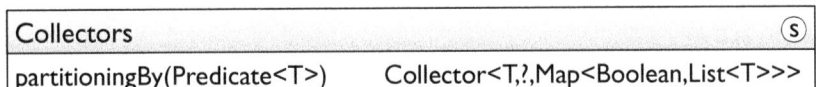

Collectors	ⓢ
partitioningBy(Predicate<T>)	Collector<T,?,Map<Boolean,List<T>>>

For example, this code would map `true` to a list of my fiction books and `false` to a list of the non-fiction ones:

```
Map<Boolean,List<Book>> fictionOrNonFiction = library.stream()
    .collect(partitioningBy(b -> b.getTopic() == FICTION ||
                                 b.getTopic() == SCIENCE_FICTION));
```

Figure 4-4 shows this example in action.

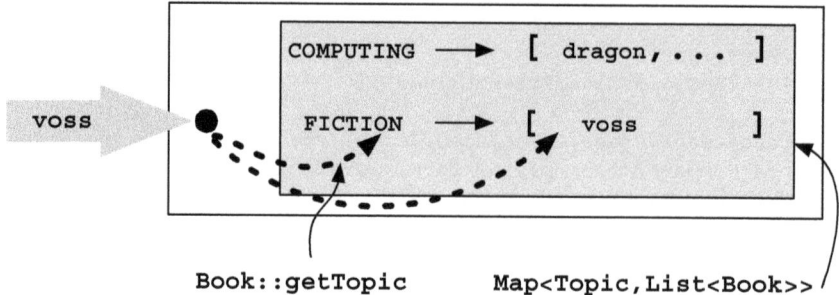

FIGURE 4-3. *How* `Collectors.groupingBy` *works*

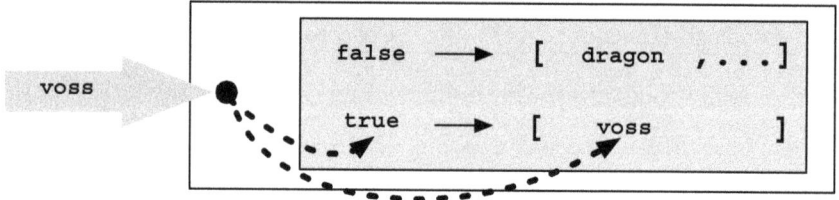

FIGURE 4-4. *How* `Collectors.partitioningBy` *works*

4.1.2 Composing Collectors

Stand-alone collectors are useful in themselves, but the real power of the Collector API lies in the way that the collectors are designed to work together and with other functions. The importance of composition in the design of Java 8 was emphasized at the beginning of Chapter 3; the Collector API provides a good example of this design principle in action.

For example, suppose we want to represent the distribution of a set of values— say, the number of books in my library on each topic. In the last section, we learned about classifying collectors, which can indeed produce mappings in which the key is a property such as the topic of a book. But the type of the value of these mappings has so far been fixed as a list of the stream elements. To represent a distribution, this list needs to be replaced with an element count. This is only one example of values that can replace a list of elements in the mapping: other possibilities include a list of derived properties of the elements (the publishers of those books, say), or other reductions over the element values (the oldest in the topic, the sum of the pages, etc.) Rather than provide specialized classifying collectors for these various use cases, the Collector API provides an extension point by allowing collectors to be composed together.

Composition allows new collectors to be created by combining the effects of two or more collectors or other operations. The most important form it takes is to allow `groupingBy` to be combined with a second, "downstream," collector. In this composition, `groupingBy` provides the classifier function and the classification keys, and and the elements associated with a given key are forwarded to the downstream collector for further summarization. Figure 4-5 shows how this works for the simple `groupingBy` overload that we already saw, in which the default downstream collector is the one returned by `Collectors.toList`.

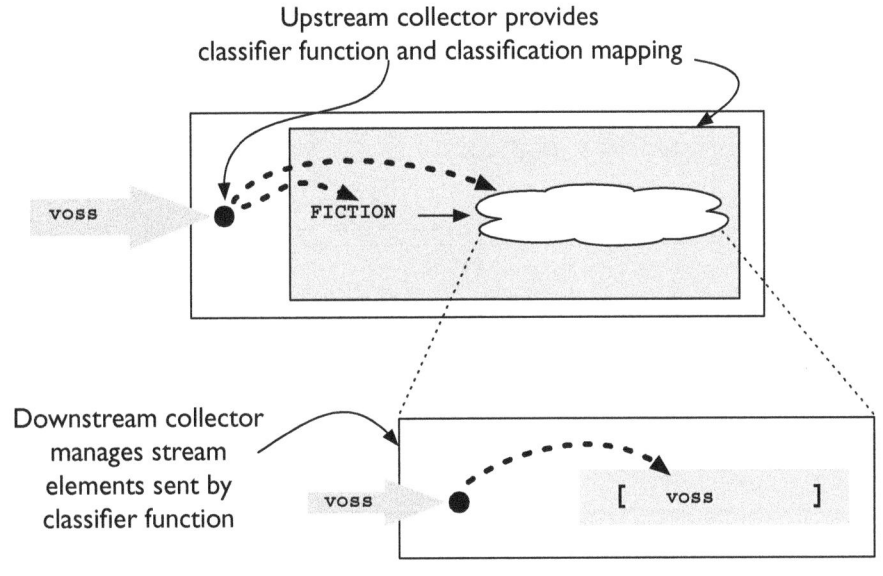

FIGURE 4-5. *groupingBy is a composition.*

A second `Collectors` factory method is provided to allow the creation of a classifying collector composed with a user-supplied downstream collector:

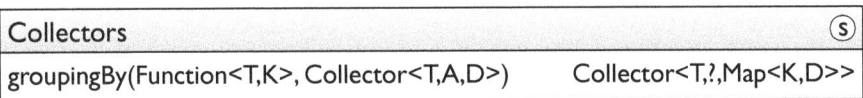

The behavior we have seen so far from `groupingBy` collectors is equivalent to using this overload to write:

```
Map<Topic,List<Book>> booksByTopic = library.stream()
    .collect(groupingBy(Book::getTopic, Collectors.toList()));
```

Returning to the example of representing a distribution, we can now see that the problem can be solved by composing `groupingBy` with a different downstream collector, one that counts the incoming elements. And, in fact, there is a `Collectors` factory method for exactly this purpose: `Collectors.counting`. (Its implementation is explained in §4.4.3). Figure 4-6 shows how it will work in this example.

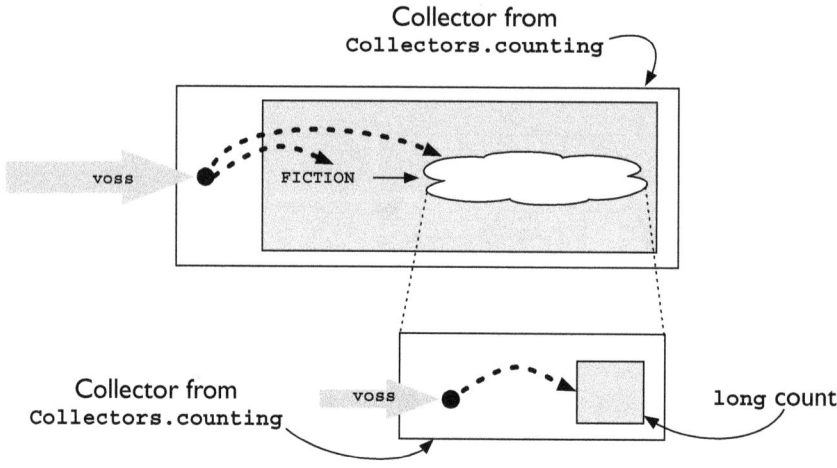

FIGURE 4-6. *Downstream to counting*

So to represent a distribution we can write

```
Map<Topic,Long> distributionByTopic = library.stream()
    .collect(groupingBy(Book::getTopic, Collectors.counting()));
```

Other collectors can be used downstream of `groupingBy`. In fact, many of the `Collectors` factory methods are designed for exactly this purpose. We can distinguish them from the stand-alone collectors of §4.1.1 by their duality with convenience reductions; for example, the collector returned by `counting` is the terminal operation `count` adapted for use as a downstream collector. For other examples:

- Corresponding to the terminal operations `max` and `min` are the `Collectors` factory methods `maxBy` and `minBy`. For example, we could create a mapping that would contain, for each topic, the book with the greatest number of authors:

```
Map<Topic,Optional<Book>> mostAuthorsByTopic = library.stream()
    .collect(groupingBy(Book::getTopic,
    maxBy(comparing(b -> b.getAuthors().size())))));
```

- Corresponding to the primitive stream terminal operations `sum` and `average` are the collectors returned by `summingInt`, `summingLong`, `summingDouble`, and their averaging analogs. For example, we could create a mapping that would contain for each topic the total number of volumes on that topic (recall that `getPageCounts` returns an array of `int` values equal in length to the number of volumes for that book):

```
Map<Topic,Integer> volumeCountByTopic = library.stream()
    .collect(groupingBy(Book::getTopic,
    summingInt(b -> b.getPageCounts().length)));
```

or one that would contain the average height of the books, by topic:

```
Map<Topic,Double> averageHeightByTopic = library.stream()
        .collect(groupingBy(Book::getTopic,
            averagingDouble(Book::getHeight)));
```

- Corresponding to the terminal operation `summaryStatistics` are collectors returned by `summarizingInt`, `summarizingLong`, and `summarizingDouble`. These collect primitive values into the corresponding `SummaryStatistics` object. For example, the following code will produce, instead of only the total count of book volumes by topic as in the last example, an `IntSummaryStatistics` instance for the stream of volume counts:

```
Map<Topic,IntSummaryStatistics> volumeStats = library.stream()
    .collect(groupingBy(Book::getTopic,
                summarizingInt(b -> b.getPageCounts().length)));
```

which we can print out using

```
System.out.println(volumeStats.get(Topic.COMPUTING));
```

to get a result like this:

```
IntSummaryStatistics{count=94, sum=98, min=1, average=1.042553, ↵
                                                        max=2}
```

- Corresponding to the three overloads of the terminal operation `reduce` are collectors returned by three overloads of the `reducing` method. We will return to these when we explore the topic of reduction at the end of this chapter.

The preceding examples all have something in common: the downstream collector—whether it is counting elements, sorting them by comparing a property, or summarizing a property—receives and has to handle the entire stream element. But sometimes a downstream collector needs to work on only a single property; for example, say that I want to create a mapping from each topic to a concatenation of all the titles in that topic. The operation of extracting the title from each book requires something very like the `map` operation on streams, but in this case applied to the stream of objects dispatched by `groupingBy` to a downstream collector before it receives them. This requirement is met by collectors created by `Collectors.mapping`, which allow the user to supply both the mapping and the downstream collector:

Collectors	Ⓢ
mapping(Function<T,U>, Collector<U,A,R>)	Collector<T,?,R>

Figure 4-7 shows how collectors created by this method work. With the help of `Collectors.mapping`, it is straightforward to create a mapping from each title to the concatenation of all titles on that topic:

```
Map<Topic,String> concatenatedTitlesByTopic = library.stream()
    .collect(groupingBy(Book::getTopic,
                    mapping(Book::getTitle, joining(";"))));
```

As a kind of dual to `mapping`, which applies a function to incoming values before they are collected, `collectingAndThen` accepts a function that it applies to the container after collection. This "finishing" operation is described further in §4.3.1.

4.1.3 Chaining Pipelines

The techniques of the last section provide different ways of processing the values for each classification key in isolation—finding a maximum value among them, concatenating the values of a string property, and so on. Some problems require a further processing stage, in which the values of different keys are processed together. Take, for example, the problem of finding the most popular topic in my library—that is, the one with the greatest number of books. We know how to produce a mapping from topic to book count:

```
Map<Topic,Long> bookCountByTopic = library.stream()
    .collect(groupingBy(Book::getTopic, counting()));
```

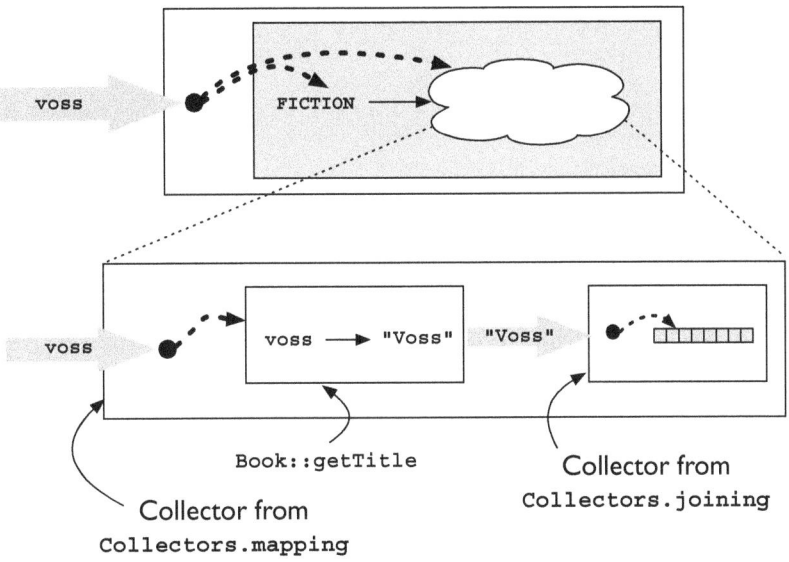

Book::getTitle

Collector from
Collectors.mapping

Collector from
Collectors.joining

FIGURE 4-7.   *groupingBy composed with* `mapping`

but now the individual entries in the `Map<Topic,Long>` have to be compared to find the one with the greatest value. Before this comparison can take place, all the elements in the library must have been processed by the collector to create the classification mapping; only then can the topic-count pairs be compared to find the one with the greatest count value. To be able to apply the operations of the Stream API to the next stage of processing, we need to start another stream having these pairs as elements:

```
Stream<Map.Entry<Topic,Long>> entries = library.stream()
    .collect(groupingBy(Book::getTopic, counting()))
    .entrySet().stream();
```

We can now work with the components of individual `Map.Entry` objects using the methods `Map.Entry.getKey` and `Map.Entry.getValue`. Java 8 added the comparator-yielding methods `comparingByKey` and `comparingByValue` for exactly this kind of situation so, for the problem of finding the most popular topic, we can write:

```
Optional<Topic> mostPopularTopic = entries
    .max(Map.Entry.comparingByValue())
    .map(Map.Entry::getKey);
```

We can imitate the fluent style of pipeline processing by chaining the two pipelines together:

```
Optional<Topic> mostPopularTopic = library.stream()
    .collect(groupingBy(Book::getTopic, counting()))
    .entrySet().stream()
    .max(Map.Entry.comparingByValue())
    .map(Map.Entry::getKey);
```

At this early stage in the adoption of Java 8, it's not possible to predict in detail how idioms will evolve. This one has advantages and disadvantages:

- It is concise and readable.

- It can be deceptive, if you aren't alert to the fact that optimizations can only be applied to the two pipelines separately and that sufficient memory will be required to hold the intermediate collection. In this, it is not actually so different from the behavior of some intermediate operations, such as `sorted`, which have to collect the entire contents of the stream internally before proceeding to the next step. We'll explore this issue further in Chapter 6.

Performance issues notwithstanding, adoption of this idiom will depend on its overall effect on readability and maintainability of code. On that basis, this book will continue to use it.

4.1.4 Worked Example: Most Popular Topics

At the end of the last section, we saw how to find the most popular topic. But that code did not take account of the possibility that there might be more than one topic with the maximum number of books and, if so, that we might want to know about all of them. In this section, we will work toward a solution of that problem; rather than simply presenting it, we will approach it in stages. At each stage, stop and think for a moment about how to go forward. To begin with, try to work out an overall approach to the problem.

One way of thinking about problems like this is to work backward from the goal. The last important step of the new program will also use `max`, as before, but the result will now include all the most popular topics instead of only one of them. That suggests they will need to be in a collection and—if this program is similar to the preceding one, so that we are seeking a maximum among map entries—leads us to look for a way of creating a `Map<Long, Set<Topic>>` (either `Set` or `List` would be a reasonable choice), in which the keys are the popularity of each topic and the value is a collection of the topics with that popularity. Following this line of reasoning, we are aiming for a mapping like this—call it `targetMap`:

```
{98=[COMPUTING, FICTION], 33=[HISTORY]}
```

And our starting point in getting to it can be the map produced by the first two lines of the previous code:

```
{COMPUTING=98, FICTION=98, HISTORY=33}
```

Call this `startMap`. How can we get from `startMap` to `targetMap`? If you have not found a solution, stop now and try to devise one. Hint: the easiest way to get between them is by using `groupingBy`.

If the goal of a `groupingBy` operation is `targetMap`, then the keys that the classifier function is extracting must be the popularities, and since they are the values in `startMap`, the classifier function must be `Map.Entry.getValue`.

The values in `targetMap` come from the keys of the `startMap` entries, so the action of the collector downstream of `groupingBy` must be first, to extract the keys from the incoming entries, and second, to accumulate them into a `Set`. This suggests composing `groupingBy` with a `mapping` collector to extract the keys, that collector itself being composed with a `toSet` collector to accumulate them:

```
startMap.entrySet().stream()
    .collect(groupingBy(Map.Entry::getValue,
                        mapping(Map.Entry::getKey, toSet())));
```

Putting everything together, the code to find the most popular topics is:

```
Optional<Set<Topic>> mostPopularTopics = library.stream()
    .collect(groupingBy(Book::getTopic, counting()))
    .entrySet().stream()
    .collect(groupingBy(Map.Entry::getValue,
                        mapping(Map.Entry::getKey, toSet())))
    .entrySet().stream()
    .max(Map.Entry.comparingByKey())
    .map(Map.Entry::getValue);
```

This is by no means the only solution to the problem. You may have considered one of a variety of alternatives:

- Insertion of `Book` elements into a sorted `Map` using `Topic` as the sort key, and retrieving an initial subset of the elements.

- Creation of a frequency map to determine the maximum value, then in a second pass accumulating the topics associated with that value.

- Defining a value object of the kind that we will see later in this chapter, and reducing directly over that.

If you can take the time to explore some of these alternatives, you will be rewarded with an appreciation of the variety of possible strategies available in this style of processing.

4.2 Anatomy of a Collector

There is a straightforward connection between recursive decomposition, as presented in Chapter 1, and collection. Recall Figure 1-2 (p. 14): the merging phase of that diagram shows how two `int` values can be combined to produce a new one, in that case the maximum of the two. That picture of classical reduction is suitable for an algorithm that always uses combination to produce new values rather than mutating existing ones, but it needs to be modified for collection to mutable containers. Figure 4-8 adapts the earlier picture to show one possible execution of this collector code:

```
Stream.of(nails, dragon, voss)
    .collect(Collectors.toList());
```

The diagram has been drawn assuming a right-to-left flow of stream elements so that they can be shown in the same order in which they appear in the source. What matters, however—at least if the stream is ordered—is that they maintain their relative position while they are being accumulated into the result container.

The conventional way of accumulating values into a collection is to create a new one, then add elements to it successively. The algorithm illustrated in the diagram adapts this inherently sequential process to parallel execution. For each thread, a supplier function creates a new container (typically a collection but, in general, anything that can accumulate references to elements or element values as, for example, `StringBuilder` does.)

Each thread can then accumulate elements into its container, using an accumulator function as in the conventional approach. Finally the intermediate containers created by the threads must be merged together; this requires a third function, the combiner, required in order to bring together the result of parallel sequential accumulation. We have not needed to learn about combiners until now, because a combiner does not change the functional behavior of a collector from what the accumulator defines (§4.3.3 makes this precise).

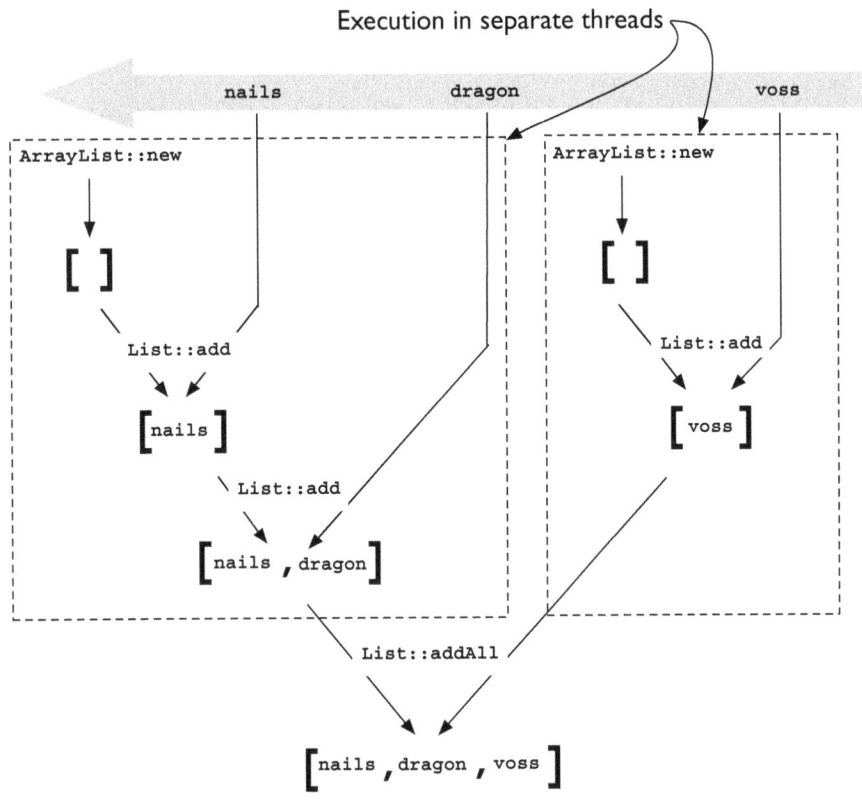

FIGURE 4-8. *Parallel mutable reduction:* `toList`

If we call the type of the stream element `T` (here `Book`) and the type of the result container `R` (here `List<Book>`), these three functions are implementations of three interfaces introduced in §2.4:

- The function to create a new container is in this case `ArrayList::new`;[1] in general it is an implementation of `Supplier<R>`.

- The function to add a single element into an existing container is in this case `List::add`; in general it is an implementation of `BiConsumer<R,T>`.

---

[1] The contract for `Collectors.toList` provides no guarantee on the type of `List` created, although in Java 8 it is in fact `ArrayList`.

- The function to combine two existing containers is in this case `List::addAll`; in general it is an implementation of `BinaryOperator<R>`.

These are the three essential components of a collector. They must work together to give consistent results—for example, it is easy to see that Figure 4-8 is only one of a number of possible executions of the code, all of which must produce the same value. In §4.3.3 we will study the rules that ensure that our custom collectors guarantee this, as the predefined collectors do.

4.2.1 Concurrent Collection

From Figure 4-8, it should be clear that the performance bottleneck in parallel stream processing is liable to be the combine operation that brings together the results of processing on separate threads. The framework guarantees that—provided a collector respects the rules of §4.3.3—accumulator operations on a given partition will only ever be executed by a single thread and that combiner operations will be executed safely, even when non-threadsafe containers are being combined. But clearly there is a performance price to pay for this safety, especially in the common case of map merging. So the framework offers an alternative: concurrent collectors.

A concurrent collector is one that has declared CONCURRENT as one of its characteristics (§6.8). This declaration informs the framework that it can safely call the accumulator function on the same result container from multiple threads. This will improve parallel performance, at the cost of losing ordering on stream elements. So the commonest use case for concurrent collection is collection to a `Map`, and every method `toMap` in the `Collectors` class has a corresponding `toConcurrentMap` method that produces a collector to a `ConcurrentMap`. Similarly, each overload of `groupingBy` has a dual `groupingByConcurrent` method returning a `ConcurrentMap` in place of a `Map`. We discuss the performance improvement that these can bring (and the circumstances under which you should use them) in §6.8.

4.3 Writing a Collector

We have seen the range of capabilities that the library's predefined collectors provide and, further, how that range can be extended by composing them together. With such a wide choice, why would you want to define your own collector? There are two possible motivations: either you need to accumulate values into a container that does not implement `Collection` (so that you cannot use `Collectors.toCollection`), or the process of accumulation requires the sharing of state between values being collected.

For a simple example of the second sort, suppose that we have a stream of values, sorted by some property, and we want to group them according to their proximity measured by that property. A physical example would be a route for a power transmission line, where the tower spacing must be no more than a constant, say MAX_DISTANCE. A potential route consisting of a series of tower sites could be analyzed by grouping the sites in segments, in each of which the towers are separated by no more than MAX_DISTANCE, whereas the distance between two towers in different segments is always greater than MAX_DISTANCE. For a very simple example (Figure 4-9), a route planned exactly along the x-axis might contain these points:

```
(3,0), (6,0), (8,0), (10,0), (14,0)
```

If MAX_DISTANCE == 2, these points would be grouped into three segments:

```
[(3.0)], [(6,0), (8,0), (10,0)], [(14,0)]
```

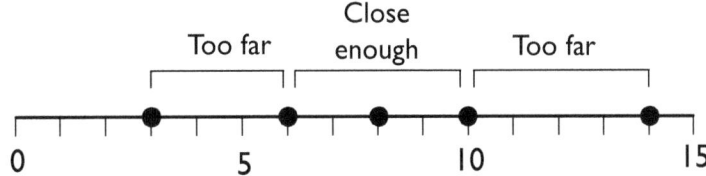

FIGURE 4-9. *Transmission tower placements*

The obvious representation for the solution to this problem is a nested linear data structure. Since adding a new element to it will require access to the last existing element, it will be convenient to use Deque rather than List as its basis; conveniently, Deque has a modern and efficient implementation in ArrayDeque.

Here is a simple iterative solution:

```
Deque<Deque<Point>> groupByProximity(List<Point> sortedPointList) {
    Deque<Deque<Point>> points = new ArrayDeque<>();
    points.add(new ArrayDeque<>());
    for (Point p : sortedPointList) {
        Deque<Point> lastSegment = points.getLast();
        if (! lastSegment.isEmpty() &&
                lastSegment.getLast().distance(p) > MAX_DISTANCE ) {
            Deque<Point> newSegment = new ArrayDeque<>();
            newSegment.add(p);
            points.add(newSegment);
        } else {
            lastSegment.add(p);
        }
    }
```

```
        }
    return points;
}
```

This is a good starting point for the collector implementation—in fact, it can serve with little modification as the basis for the accumulator. The combiner is more of a challenge: its function is to merge two `Deque` instances, each representing a solution over part of the input. There are two possibilities for the merge, depending on the distance between the last point in the left part and the first point in the right part. If these are sufficiently close, the last left segment and the first right segment must be merged; otherwise the right part can be simply appended to the left.

Here are definitions of the three components—supplier, accumulator, and combiner—of the collector:

- A supplier can often simply be the constructor for the container; it is tempting to write `ArrayDeque::new` here. But the correct initial value is an empty container, ready for use by the accumulator or combiner. In this case that is a single empty segment:

```
Supplier<Deque<Deque<Point>>> supplier =
    () -> {
        Deque<Deque<Point>> ddp = new ArrayDeque<>();
        ddp.add(new ArrayDeque<>());
        return ddp;
    }
```

- The accumulator has the same task as in the sequential code, that of adding a single `Point` to a partial solution:

```
BiConsumer<Deque<Deque<Point>>,Point> accumulator =
    (ddp, p) -> {
        Deque<Point> last = ddp.getLast();
        if (! last.isEmpty()
                && last.getLast().distance(p) > MAX_DISTANCE ) {
            Deque<Point> dp = new ArrayDeque<>();
            dp.add(p);
            ddp.add(dp);
        } else {
            last.add(p);
        }
    }
```

- The combiner merges two partial solutions, as discussed above:

```
BinaryOperator<Deque<Deque<Point>>,
    Deque<Deque<Point>>> combiner =
    (left, right) -> {
        Deque<Point> leftLast = left.getLast();
        if (leftLast.isEmpty()) return right;
        Deque<Point> rightFirst = right.getFirst();
        if (rightFirst.isEmpty()) return left;
        Point p = rightFirst().getFirst();
        if (leftLast.getLast().distance(p) <= MAX_DISTANCE ) {
            leftLast.addAll(rightFirst);
            right.removeFirst();
        }
        left.addAll(right);
        return left;
    }
```

Figure 4-10 shows the supplier, the accumulator, and the combiner working together on one possible execution of the sample input from p. 91.

These three functions can be assembled into a `Collector` using the factory method `Collector.of`. The `Characteristics` parameter to `Collector.of` is a way of supplying performance-related metadata about the collector (§6.8):

Collector<T,A,R>	ⓢ
of(Supplier<A>, BiConsumer<A,T>, BinaryOperator<A>, Characteristics...) Collector<T,A,R>	

Now all that is needed to realize Figure 4-10 is to call `Collector.of` and supply the resulting collector to `Stream.collect`:

```
Deque<Deque<Point>> displacementRecords = sortedPointList.stream()
    .collect(Collector.of(supplier, accumulator, combiner));
```

Performance   This collector parallelizes well. Its performance characteristics are examined in more detail in 6.8.2, but the discussion can be summarized as follows: executed sequentially, its performance is very close to that of the iterative version shown earlier. Terminating a stream with no intermediate operation costs, the parallel speedup is a factor of about 1.8 on a 4-core machine; as the intermediate operations become more expensive, the relative parallel speedup improves.

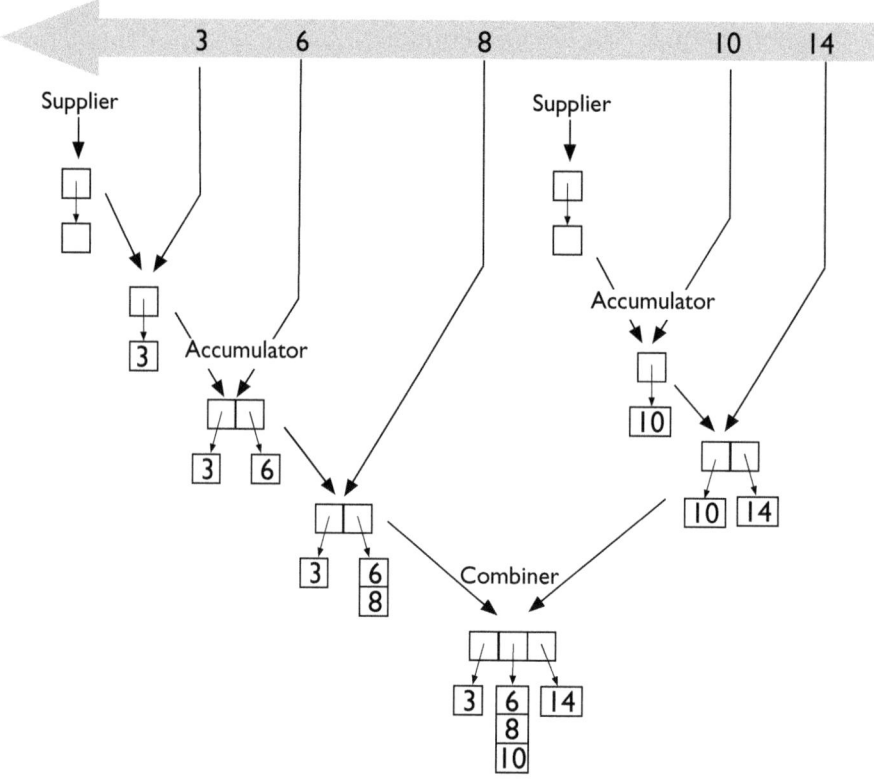

FIGURE 4-10. *Collection* `Point` *instances by proximity*

4.3.1 Finishers

The discussion of collector composition mentioned in passing (p. 84) the method `col-lectingAndThen`, which accepts a function to be applied to the container after collection is complete:

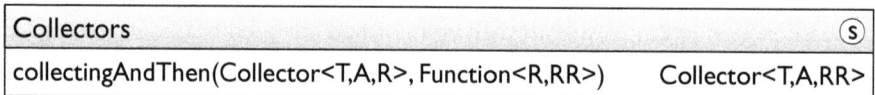

Collectors	Ⓢ
collectingAndThen(Collector<T,A,R>, Function<R,RR>)	Collector<T,A,RR>

This method allows you to provide an additional finishing transformation on the container produced by the collector. For example, to obtain an immutable list of book titles we could adapt the collector returned by `toList` by writing:

```
List<String> titles = library.stream()
    .map(Book::getTitle)
    .collect(collectingAndThen(toList(),
                                Collections::unmodifiableList));
```

There are several reasons why a finishing function could be required:

- The intermediate container is of the wrong type to be returned (for example, the `StringBuilder` used internally in `joining`).

- Some processing has to be deferred until all the elements have been seen, such as computing an average.

- The result should be returned in a canonical form, for example, by rebalancing a tree.

- The result must be "sealed" in some way before being returned, for example with an unmodifiable or synchronized wrapper.

Some collectors always require a finisher for their operation. An example is provided by `joining`, implemented by a collector although its result type is `String`, which—as an immutable type—is unsuitable for collection. (Later we will see a reduction form that could be used instead, but that would perform very poorly in the course of concatenating strings for every accumulation or combination operation.) In fact, the container for `joining` is the mutable type `StringBuilder`; conversion to `String` only takes place in the finishing function, after the reduction is complete. As this finisher is always needed, it should be built into the collector; there is an overload of `Collector.of` for that purpose:

Collector<T,A,R>   (S)
of(Supplier<A> supplier,
BiConsumer<A,T> accumulator,
BinaryOperator<A> combiner,
Function<A,R> finisher,
Characteristics... characteristics
)   Collector<T,A,R>

This finally makes sense of the second type parameter of `Collector`: it is the type of the intermediate container into which accumulation takes place. When we use a collector, we don't have to concern ourselves with this type, which relates only to the collector's internal mechanism; and often in writing one, we may just use the output type, as in the example of the previous section. In the next example (§4.3.2), we have a choice between using a finishing function to convert the output of the combiner to the desired type or of applying a `map` operation subsequently.

To visualize a built-in finisher, consider this code to create a stream of strings, each containing all the authors' names for a single book:

```
Stream<String> concatenatedAuthors = library.stream()
    .map(b -> b.getAuthors().stream().collect(joining());
```

Figure 4-11 shows successive stages in its execution. In part (a) the characters in the input strings are accumulated in the internal `StringBuilder` object that is being built up; in part (b) the input stream is exhausted, the finisher function is applied to the intermediate object, and the resulting `String` is returned.

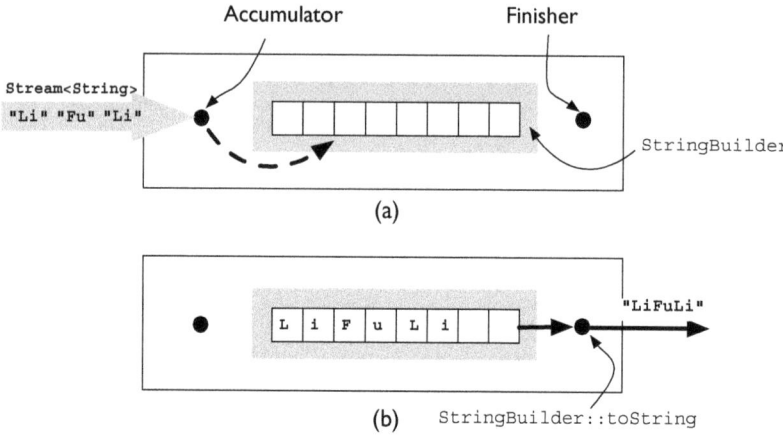

FIGURE 4-11.   *How* `Collectors.joining` *works*

Embedding finishing functions into collectors makes them suitable as downstream collectors to `groupingBy` in a way that they would not be if the finisher had to be applied separately. For example, consider this code to create a mapping from each letter to the concatenation of all book titles beginning with that letter:

```
Map<Character, String> collect1 = library.stream()
    .map(Book::getTitle)
    .collect(groupingBy(t -> t.charAt(0), joining(";")));
```

If the finisher for `joining` were not part of the collector but had to be applied separately, after the collection by `groupingBy` had taken place, it would be necessary to iterate over the resulting map, applying the finisher to each value. Instead, the joining finisher is available to be composed into the groupingBy finisher, to be applied by it to each value of the classification mapping.

4.3.2 Worked Example: Finding My Books

This section extends the discussion of collectors with a slightly more complex example, in which we will work out how to compute the position of each book on my shelves, assuming that they are arranged in alphabetical order of title. I know how many pages each book has and how thick each page is, so if I could create a map from each book title to the total page count of its predecessors on the shelf, I could easily calculate the displacement of each book from the start of the shelf. This is another example of a state-sharing problem, but somewhat harder to solve (and more expensive to compute): each value in the map, except the first, depends on its predecessors.

A major difficulty in solving this problem is in opening your mind to different solutions: every Java developer has written many programs that initialize properties like cumulative displacements, then accumulate changes to them by iterating over data like individual page counts. This is such a familiar pattern that it is tempting to jump to the conclusion that any algorithms for such problems must be sequential. Here we want to break down that assumption by investigating an alternative that uses reduction: that way, we should get a better program, focusing on the essentials of the problem, that may also be a faster program, avoiding contention.

The key step in designing a recursive algorithm like this is devising a data structure to hold partial results so that successive applications of the combiner can eventually merge these together into the final output. But the combiner will also need the input corresponding to the partial results, so the data structure must represent both of these together.

Stop reading for a moment and think about the design of this data structure.

The partial results for a single book is the title-displacement pair, and the partial input associated with that is the page count for the book. That leads to the definition of a helper class:

```
class DispRecord {
    final String title;
    final int disp, length;
    DispRecord(String t, int d, int l) {
        this.title = t; this.disp = d; this.length = l;
    }
    int totalDisp() { return disp + length; }
}
```

This example will illustrate why there is so much enthusiasm for the (very long-term) project of introducing tuples to the Java language. Value class declarations are verbose and potentially inefficient compared to the implementation of value objects as tuples in other languages. That said, we can at least make the best of a bad job: the ability to define convenience methods like `totalDisp` is some compensation for having to use a value class.

The problem specifies an unordered map from title to displacement, but the calculation of each `DispRecord` relies on its predecessor, so an ordered container will be required during the collection process. We'll use `Deque` for this purpose, again in order to take advantage of its convenient provision of access to its last element.

We are now ready to write the components of the collector:

- The supplier is easy to define: in this case, all that is needed is to create an empty container, via `ArrayDeque::new`:

```
Supplier<Deque<DispRecord>> supplier = ArrayDeque::new;
```

- The accumulator is only a little more difficult: its task is to add a `DispRecord` to the end of an existing `Deque`. Stop again and outline the code for this.

The accumulator appends a single `Book` to a `Deque<DispRecord>`, calculating its displacement from the last element of the deque by adding its displacement to its page count.

```
BiConsumer<Deque<DispRecord>,Book> accumulator =
    (dqLeft, b) -> {
        int disp = dqLeft.isEmpty() ? 0 :
            dqLeft.getLast().totalDisp();
        dqLeft.add(new DispRecord(b.getTitle(),
            disp,
            Arrays.stream(b.getPageCounts()).sum())));
    };
```

- Now for the combiner. This has the task of merging two `Deque<DispRecord>` instances. If you have not already worked it out, stop now to write or outline the code.

The combiner must increase the displacement field of each of the elements in the second one by the total page count of the elements in the first one. This can be calculated from the last of these, again by adding its displacement to its page count. Then the two collections can be merged:

```
BinaryOperator<Deque<DispRecord>> combiner =
        (left, right) -> {
            if (left.isEmpty()) return right;
            int newDisp = left.getLast().totalDisp();
            List<DispRecord> displacedRecords = right.stream()
                .map(dr -> new DispRecord(
                        dr.title, dr.disp + newDisp, dr.length))
                .collect(toList());
            left.addAll(displacedRecords);
            return left;
        };
```

Now the main objective of the problem is achieved—the book displacements are calculated—but the results are not exactly in the form required by the problem specification, which demanded a mapping from book title to displacement. One way of implementing this requirement is to stream the output from the collector we have just defined into a further collector created by `Collectors.toMap`. The alternative is to add a finisher to the existing collector. Stop for the last time on this problem to think how a suitable finisher could be defined, and what other change would be required.

In this case, the work of the finisher is just to create a `Map` from its input. By the time the finisher is invoked, however, the fork/join threads will have completed work on the combiner, so should be available for a concurrent map merge:

```
Function<Deque<DispRecord>,Map<String,Integer>> finisher =
        ddr -> ddr.parallelStream().collect(
            toConcurrentMap(dr -> dr.title, dr -> dr.disp));
```

Figure 4-12 shows the four functions we have defined working together on our three sample books from Chapter 3.

All that is needed to realize Figure 4-12 is to call `Collector.of` and supply the resulting collector to `Stream.collect`:

```
Map<String,Integer> displacementMap = library.stream()
    .collect(Collector.of(supplier, accumulator, combiner, finisher));
```

Performance   The different factors that contribute to the performance of this program make it an interesting example; §6.8.3 analyzes them in some detail. To briefly summarize that discussion: as it stands, the program is slower than the iterative version,

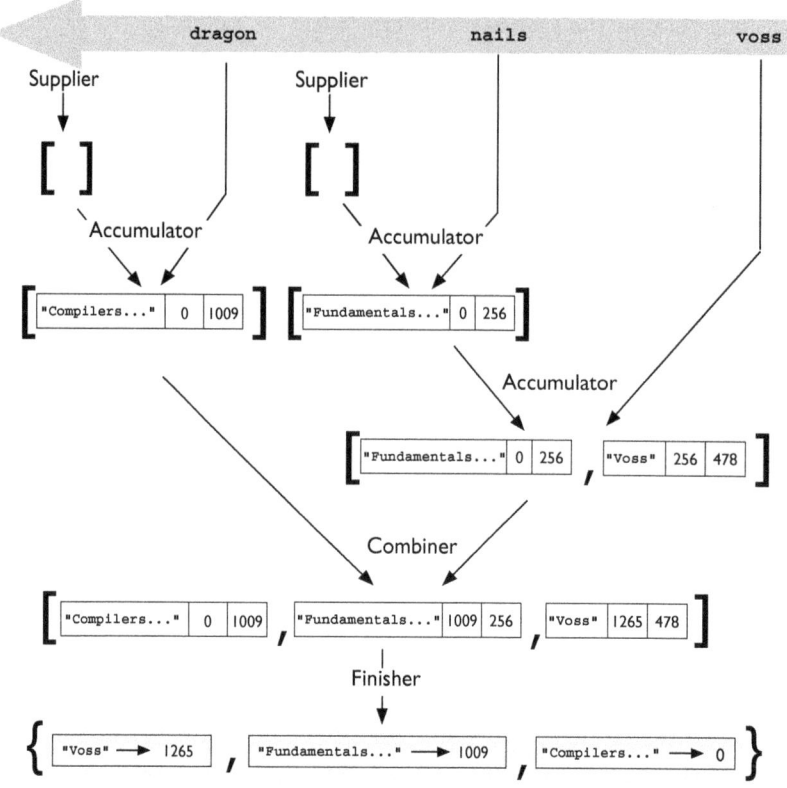

FIGURE 4-12. *Collecting book displacements*

for a number of reasons: it is an example of a *prefix sum*, in which the value of every element depends on the values of the preceding ones. In a naïve parallel algorithm for prefix sum, like this one, the total cost of the combine operations is proportional to the size of the input data set, regardless of the level of parallelism in use.[2] The combine operation used here is quite expensive (unnecessarily so, in fact). A second problem is caused by the expense of the map merge performed by the finisher; this can be mitigated by presizing the map. A third problem is the low per-element workload of the program—in real-life situations, preprocessing before collection will usually be

---

[2] Java 8 provided `java.util.Arrays` with various overloads of a new method `parallelPrefix` for computing prefix sums efficiently, but this innovation has not yet reached the Stream API.

required. Whether these problems make this program unsuitable for parallelization is discussed in §6.8.3.

4.3.3 Rules for Collectors

When a collector is executed in the way pictured in Figure 4-12, a complex interplay takes place between the framework and the collector-supplied components. For this to work correctly, each side must be able to rely on the other obeying certain rules. This section lays those rules down: what a collector can expect from the framework, and the constraints it must itself respect.

The framework guarantees to respect the following conditions:

- New values will appear only as the second argument to the accumulator; all other values will be results previously returned from supplier, accumulator, or combiner.

- Results from the supplier, accumulator, and combiner may be returned to the caller of `collect`; otherwise, they will only ever be used as arguments to the accumulator, combiner, or finisher.

- Values passed to the combiner or finisher and not returned are never used again; their contents have been processed and should not be reused.

The collector must respect the following constraints:

- Unless it has the characteristic CONCURRENT (see §4.2.1), it must ensure that any result returned from the supplier, accumulator, or combiner functions is thread-confined (i.e., it must not have been made available to any other thread). This enables the collector framework to parallelize processing without being concerned about interference from external threads.

- If it has the characteristic CONCURRENT, the accumulator must be threadsafe using the same concurrently modifiable result container, as the framework may call it concurrently from multiple threads. Concurrent collectors cannot be used when ordering is significant.

- The identity constraint: the empty result container should leave other elements unchanged when combined with them. More formally, for any value of s:

```
s == combiner.apply(s, supplier.get())
s == combiner.apply(supplier.get(), s)
```

- The associativity constraint: splitting the computation in different places should produce the same result. More formally, for any values of q, r, and s:

```
combiner.apply(combiner.apply(q, r), s)) ==
                        combiner.apply(q, combiner.apply(r, s))
```

- The compatibility constraint: dividing the computation in different ways between the accumulator and combiner should produce the same result. More formally, for any values of r, s, and t, the same value of r should result from executing the two lines of code on the left as the two on the right:

```
accumulator.accept(s, t);      r = combiner.apply(r, s);
r = combiner.apply(r, s);      accumulator.accept(r, t);
```

4.4 Reduction

At the start of this chapter, a comparison between collection and its special case, reduction, came out in favor of collection as more generally useful in Java programs. However, reduction is useful in some circumstances; in this section, we will explore the uses of reduction as implemented by the Stream API.

4.4.1 Reduction over Primitives

We already saw (p. 66) convenience methods provided for special-purpose reductions on primitive streams, including sum, min, max, count, and average. In this section, we will see how these relate to the general capabilities of the reduce method and how it can be used to define new functions over streams of primitives. The examples in this section use IntStream, but the other primitive stream classes have exactly analogous methods.

The basic idea of reduction over primitives follows the same divide-and-conquer approach that led us to identify the three components of a collector from Figure 4-8. Using the form of that figure for a simple reduction over primitives—summation over int values—gives us Figure 4-13, representing the code

```
int sumResult = IntStream.of(1,2,3)
    .sum();
```

This figure has two significant differences from the collector diagram:

- A base value—the *identity* for the reduction—is used in place of empty container instances created by a supplier function in the earlier figure.

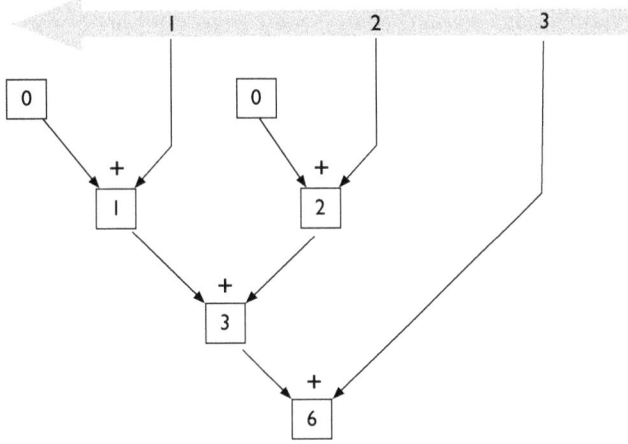

FIGURE 4-13.   *Primitive reduction*

- The accumulator and combiner are the same, because only one type is involved.

This helps to clarify the signature of the second overload of `IntStream.reduce`:

IntStream	ⓘ
reduce(IntBinaryOperator)	OptionalInt
reduce(int, IntBinaryOperator)	int

If the convenience method `sum` were not available, we could write code to implement Figure 4-13 using the second overload of `reduce`:

```
int sum = IntStream.of(1,2,3)
    .reduce(0, (a, b) -> a + b);
```

Of the convenience methods that we saw in §3.2.4, `sum`, `count`, and `average` are derived in this way from `reduce`. New functions can be similarly defined: for example, the following code computes the factorial of a variable `intArg`:

```
int intArgFactorial = IntStream.rangeClosed(1, intArg)
    .reduce(1, (a, b) -> a * b);
```

Given an empty stream, this variant of `reduce` returns the supplied identity. By contrast, the first overload of `reduce` does not accept an identity and so, given an empty stream, must return an empty `OptionalInt`. This is the variant used to define the convenience methods `max` and `min`. If they were not part of the API, we could use the one-argument version of `IntStream.reduce` to obtain the same effect. For example:

```
OptionalInt min = IntStream.of(1,2,3)
    .reduce((a, b) -> Math.min(a,b));
```

One execution of this code is shown in Figure 4-14.

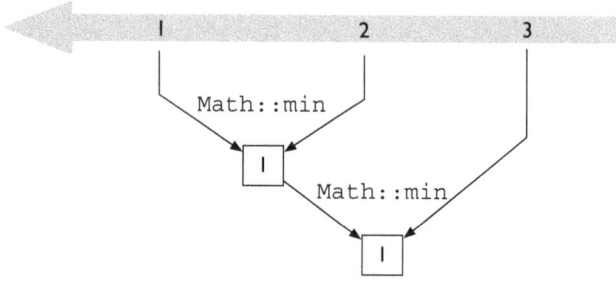

FIGURE 4-14. *Primitive reduction without an identity*

4.4.2 Reduction over Reference Streams

After collection and reduction over primitives, reduction over reference streams looks quite familiar: two of the overloads of `Stream.reduce` are similar to `reduce` on primitive streams, and—perhaps confusingly—the third one has a superficial similarity to collection, although its use is very different:

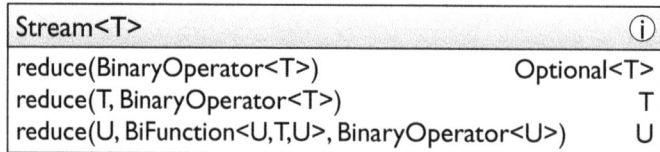

Stream<T>	ⓘ
reduce(BinaryOperator<T>)	Optional<T>
reduce(T, BinaryOperator<T>)	T
reduce(U, BiFunction<U,T,U>, BinaryOperator<U>)	U

We now consider each of these three overloads in turn. The first accepts only a combiner without an identity and so, analogously to the single-argument primitive `reduce`, returns an `Optional`. It is useful in several different situations: one is where a binary operator, like `Comparator.compare`, returns one of its operands. For example, we could find the first book title in alphabetic order by writing

```
Comparator<Book> titleComparator = Comparator.comparing(Book::getTitle);
Optional<Book> first = library.stream()
    .reduce(BinaryOperator.minBy(titleComparator));
```

In fact, this is how the convenience reduction method `Stream.min` (p. 66) is implemented. Execution of this code can be visualized in the same way as the corresponding reduction over primitives (Figure 4-14). A binary operator could also return a newly created object, for example the result of calling one of the binary arithmetic operators on `BigInteger` or `BigDecimal` (notice that we choose these types as examples for reduction because they are immutable):

```
Stream<BigInteger> biStream = LongStream.of(1,2,3)
    .mapToObj(BigInteger::valueOf);
Optional<BigInteger> bigIntegerSum = biStream
    .reduce(BigInteger::add);
```

The combiner in all three overloads of `reduce` must respect the same associativity constraint as for the combiner of a collector and for the same reason: that different executions splitting a computation in different places must nevertheless return the same results. So, for all values of q, r, and s:

```
combiner.apply(combiner.apply(q, r), s) ==
                              combiner.apply(q, combiner.apply(r, s))
```

The remaining two overloads of `Stream.reduce` require an identity. The object used for this must not be mutated by the accumulator or combiner, as `reduce` may reuse the same object repeatedly—in contrast to collection, where the `Supplier` creates a new object at every call.

The first of these two accepts an identity and a binary operator. We could use it in an alternative to the single-argument overload to sum a `BigInteger` stream without needing to return an `Optional`:

```
BigInteger bigIntegerSum = biStream
    .reduce(BigInteger.ZERO, BigInteger::add);
```

Notice again the similarity of this to reduction over primitives; it is only appropriate with an immutable identity like `BigInteger.ZERO`. Execution of this code can again be visualized in the same way as the corresponding reduction over primitives (Figure 4-13).

Again, as with collectors, the combiner must respect the identity constraint: given any s and the identity id

```
        s == combiner.apply(s, id) == combiner.apply(id, s)
```

The third overload introduces an accumulator, and with it the possibility of returning a different type, for example an aggregate of some kind. Here it is used to calculate the total number of volumes in my library (as illustrated in Figure 4-15):

```
int totalVolumes = library.stream()
    .reduce(0,
            (sum, book) -> sum + book.getPageCounts().length,
            Integer::sum);
```

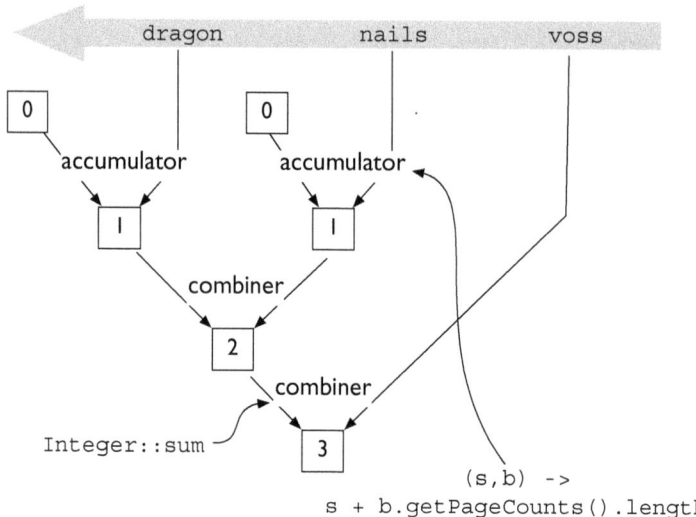

FIGURE 4-15. *Long-form reduction*

Notice that you can (and normally would) write this code as separate map and reduce operations:

```
int totalVolumes = library.stream()
    .mapToInt(b -> b.getPageCounts().length)
    .sum();
```

However, this overload of `reduce` is provided for those situations in which significant optimization can be achieved by combining mapping and reducing into a single function.

Once again, as with collectors, the accumulator and combiner functions must be compatible, to ensure that all possible executions of a program will give the same result, however the computation is divided between them. The situation is simpler here, however (things are always simpler without mutation!): for all values of r, s, and t, the following equality must hold:

```
combiner(r, accumulator(s, t)) == accumulator(combiner(r, s), t)
```

To conclude this section, we should reconsider the claim with which the chapter began, that collection was likely to prove more useful than reduction in Java programming with streams. The fact that the overloads with identity cannot accumulate into mutable types definitely makes them less valuable than collection. But the single-argument overload of reduce can serve the same purpose as collection, if it is combined with a preliminary mapping stage. For the purpose of comparison, this section concludes with a reduction solution to the cumulative page count problem already solved by collection (§4.3). Figure 4-16 shows a visualization of the program; compare it with Figure 4-12 to see the difference in the two approaches.

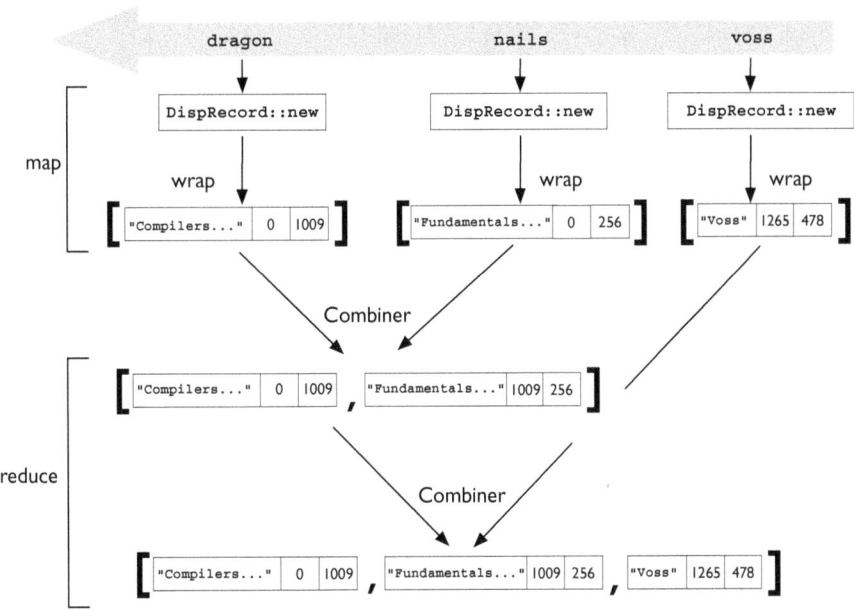

FIGURE 4-16.   *Cumulative book displacement (map-reduce version)*

Figure 4-16 is divided into two parts, labeled "map" and "reduce". The map section does the work of the supplier and accumulator components of the collection version; first it creates a `DispRecord` for each `Book` using a new constructor:

```
DispRecord(Book b) {
    this(b.getTitle(), 0, IntStream.of(b.getPageCounts()).sum());
}
```

then wrapping this in a single-element `Deque` using a helper method `wrap`:

```
Deque<DispRecord> wrap(DispRecord dr) {
    Deque<DispRecord> ddr = new ArrayDeque<>();
    ddr.add(dr);
    return ddr;
}
```

The reduce section is the same as the combiner in the collection version (p. 99).

Finally, the client code has more work to do: in this version, it must compose the map and reduce stages, as well as explicitly handle the case of an empty stream, rather than delegating everything to the collector as before:

```
Map<String, Integer> displacementMap = library.stream()
    .map(DispRecord::new)
    .map(this::wrap)
    .reduce(combiner).orElseGet(ArrayDeque::new)
    .stream()
    .collect(toMap(dr -> dr.title, dr -> dr.disp));
```

4.4.3 Composing Collectors with Reduction

In §4.1.2 we saw examples of a number of "downstream" collectors—with functions dual to various terminal operations—provided for composition with other collectors. Among them were mentioned three overloads of the `reducing` method, returning collectors corresponding to the three overloads of `Stream.reduce`. Now that we understand `Stream.reduce`, we can return to reconsider them briefly:

Collectors	ⓢ
reducing(BinaryOperator<T>)	Collector<T,?,Optional<T>>
reducing(T, BinaryOperator<T>)	Collector<T,?,T>
reducing(U, Function<T,U>, BinaryOperator<U>)	Collector<T,?,U>

These collectors are used for the same reasons as their corresponding `reduce` overloads, but in a downstream context, typically downstream of a `groupingBy` collector. For example, to find the tallest book in each topic, we could use the first overload:

```
Comparator<Book> htComparator = Comparator.comparing(Book::getHeight);
Map<Topic,Optional<Book>> maxHeightByTopic = library.stream()
    .collect(groupingBy(Book::getTopic,
                    reducing(BinaryOperator.maxBy(htComparator))));
```

The three-argument overload is used in a similar way. Notice, however, that instead of an accumulator, this overload expects a `Function<T,U>`, similar in intent to the mapping stage of the book displacement example of the previous section. For example, I could calculate the number of volumes in each topic of my library using this overload:

```
Map<Topic,Integer> volumesByTopic = library.stream()
    .collect(groupingBy(Book::getTopic,
        reducing(0, b -> b.getPageCounts().length, Integer::sum)));
```

The factory method `Collector.counting` is implemented using this overload. For example, if it were not provided, I could count the number of books in each topic of my library like this:

```
Map<Topic,Long> booksByTopic = library.stream()
    .collect(groupingBy(Book::getTopic,
                    reducing(0L, e -> 1L, Long::sum)));
```

4.5 Conclusion

In this chapter we have explored what Stream API offers for summarizing the results of stream processing. These fall into two categories: reduction and collection. The role of reduction is for summarizing immutable values, and the Stream API provides various convenience methods to support reduction, particularly over primitives.

However, the most important technique is collection, a generalization of reduction that adapts it to concurrent accumulation into mutable collections, managing access even to those that are not threadsafe. We reviewed library collectors for accumulation to standard library collections, to custom collections, and to classification mappings. Since the collector pattern lends itself to composition, the library also contains a number of collectors specifically designed to be composed with others. Further, the API provides extension points to allow the development of custom collectors where necessary, and we have seen examples of situations that call for these and techniques for developing them. Overall, collection is a powerful and flexible tool. Mastering its possibilities is central to becoming expert in using the Stream API.

That concludes our investigation of how streams can be ended; in the next chapter, we will turn our attention to the dual problem of how they can be started.

CHAPTER
5

Starting Streams: Sources
and Spliterators

C hapter 3 briefly introduced the subject of stream sources in general, but the subsequent stream processing examples have all used either collections or stream factory methods for their source. This reflects the expected mainstream usage, but it is now time to explore other aspects of stream creation. In this chapter we will cover

- Stream-bearing methods of the platform classes

- Treatment of exceptions thrown by stream sources and in intermediate operations

- The mechanism by which stream sources work

- An example bringing these topics together

5.1 Creating Streams

After the stream-bearing methods of the `Collection` interface (see p. 50), perhaps the most important ways of creating streams are the factory methods of the stream interfaces themselves. Of these, `Stream.empty` and `Stream.of` were also introduced in Chapter 3. The next group consists of `iterate` and `generate`:

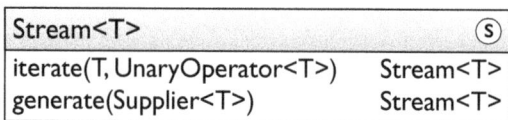

Stream<T>	ⓢ
iterate(T, UnaryOperator<T>)	Stream<T>
generate(Supplier<T>)	Stream<T>

The method `iterate` accepts a seed and a function (represented by the functional interface `UnaryOperator`) and repeatedly applies the function to produce successive stream elements. Analogous `iterate` methods are declared by all the primitive streams. Primitive streams have analogous methods. For example, to create a sequential ordered `IntStream` that will deliver alternating values of 1 and –1 indefinitely, we could write:

```
IntStream alternatingSigns = IntStream.iterate(1, i -> -i);
```

Each element in the stream is produced by applying the function to the preceding element. Streams produced by `iterate` are infinite: you get useful results from them only by using an operation that can be applied to a finite initial substream, like `limit` and the short-circuit "search" operations (p. 63).

The method `generate` takes a `Supplier`, representing a function that produces a value without requiring input, and repeatedly calls it to produce successive stream elements. The resulting sequential stream is not ordered, so `generate` is intended for use in situations where a series of values is within a distribution rather than sequentially related. For example, it can be used to generate constant streams or custom random distributions.

Factory methods in the third group create an ordered stream containing a range of values. They are defined only on the integral primitive types `IntStream` and `LongStream`. These are the `IntStream` versions:

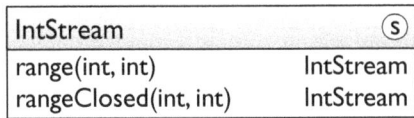

The API includes both `range` and `rangeClosed` in order to accommodate conflicting expectations about whether a range should include or exclude the specified end value. So the same stream can be created in two different ways; for example:

```
IntStream.range(1, 6).forEach(System.out::print);        //prints 12345
IntStream.rangeClosed(1, 5).forEach(System.out::print);  //prints 12345
```

One application of these methods is in the simulation of indexed streams. These are not directly supported in the Stream API but, by mapping elements of `IntStream.range` and `IntStream.rangeClosed` against indexed collections or arrays, we can achieve the same effect. Suppose, for example, that I want a listing of the books in my library showing the volume numbers and page counts of each, like this:

```
Fundamentals of Chinese Fingernail Image: 1:256
Compilers: Principles, Techniques and Tools: 1:1009
Voss: 1:478
Lord of the Rings: 1:531, 2:416, 3:624
```

I could use `IntStream.rangeClosed` to achieve this effect:

```
library.stream()
    .map(book -> {
        int[] volumes = book.getPageCounts();
        return
            IntStream.rangeClosed(1, volumes.length)
                .mapToObj(i -> i + ":" + volumes[i - 1])
                .collect(joining(", ", book.getTitle() + ": ", ""));
    })
    .forEach(System.out::println);
```

This technique, of using the elements of an `int` range as an index, can be extended to multiple data sources, providing a workaround for the absence in the Stream API of an operation to "zip" two streams together.

The last `Stream` method, not a stream creator but a stream combinator, is the static method `concat`, which creates a new stream from the concatenation of two existing ones:

Stream<T>	Ⓢ
concat(Stream<T>, Stream<T>) Stream<T>	

The rest of this section lists the methods that have been added to other platform classes to expose their data for processing in the new style.

java.util.Arrays   This class has methods to stream arrays of reference types and each of the primitive stream types. For each stream type there are two overloads, the first one streaming the entire array and the second streaming a slice of the array defined by an inclusive start and exclusive end index.

Arrays	Ⓢ
stream(T[ ])	Stream<T>
stream(T[ ], int, int)	Stream<T>
stream(int[ ])	IntStream
stream(int[ ], int, int)	IntStream
stream(long[ ])	LongStream
stream(long[ ], int, int)	LongStream
stream(double[ ])	DoubleStream
stream(double[ ], int, int)	DoubleStream

It appears that the methods accepting an entire array (rather than a slice) overlap in function with the various specializations of `Stream.of`, whose varargs parameter can be passed an array argument. However, `Stream.of` is really intended for the case when you want to supply a fixed and known number of arguments, and a call supplying an array is, in effect, arbitrarily interpreted as a series of individual values to be streamed rather than as a single array. Avoid this minor problem by favoring `Arrays.stream` for array arguments.

java.io.BufferedReader   This class reads text files; prior to Java 8, its principal usage was through the method `readLine`, which returns one line per call. In Java 8, it now also declares the method `lines`:

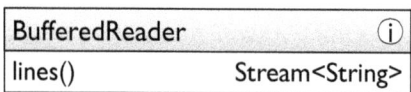

BufferedReader	ⓘ
lines()	Stream<String>

This method populates the stream lazily, by calling `BufferedReader.readLine` as and when values are required by downstream operations. It is not intended to work in conjunction with any other operation, so the reader cannot be otherwise accessed while the stream's terminal operation is executing, and no assumptions can be made about its state after the terminal operation has completed. If you want to continue to use the reader after calling `lines`, you must first reset it to a previously set mark.

The `BufferedReader` methods called by `lines` can throw `IOException` under various error conditions, for example when the reader has been closed. Rather than forcing the caller to handle these checked exceptions, `lines` wraps them in an `UncheckedIOException`, which is thrown from the terminal operation that triggered the read. We'll explore the effects of this in the next section.

In Chapter 6 we will see that among the factors influencing the performance of parallel streams is the concurrency level achievable by the source. The delivery of data from a streaming source like `BufferedReader` is inherently sequential, so the library strategy for splitting it is to divide it into batches as it becomes available. If reading the data in this way is the most expensive part of processing, then parallelism will provide little benefit. However, if the spliterator can buffer the data before splitting, it may be able to keep parallel streams supplied with data. We'll see a useful alternative to sequential file reading in the worked example at the end of this chapter.

`java.nio.file.Files` This class provides operations on files and directories, usually by delegation to the native file system. To maintain consistency with pre-existing methods of the class, these methods throw `IOException` if a file cannot be opened, but all subsequent `IOException`s are wrapped in an `UncheckedIOException`, as with `BufferedReader`.

The first group of four methods produce directory listings in stream form:

Files	(S)
walk(Path, FileVisitOption...)	Stream\<Path>
walk(Path, int, FileVisitOption...)	Stream\<Path>
find(Path, int, BiPredicate\<Path,BasicFileAttributes>, FileVisitOption...)	Stream\<Path>
list(Path)	Stream\<Path>

The listings produced by `walk` and `find` are recursive—that is, they include all subdirectories of the start directory; those produced by `list` are for the start directory only. The recursive methods take zero or more arguments of the type `FileVisitOption`, an enum that allows the traversal to be configured, for example by specifying whether symbolic links should be followed. Otherwise, they differ in whether to support a maximum traversal depth and whether to accept a predicate that filters paths for acceptability based on their `BasicFileAttributes` (such as modification, access time, or size).

The streams returned from these methods indirectly encapsulate native file handles, so it is good practice to allocate them in a try-with-resources construct. For example, the following code recursively descends the directory tree, starting from the current directory, printing some details about each file:

```
Path start = new File(".").toPath();
try(Stream<Path> pathStream = Files.walk(start)) {
    pathStream
        .map(Path::toFile)
        .filter(File::isFile)
        .map(f -> f.getAbsolutePath() + " " + f.length())
        .forEachOrdered(System.out::println);
} catch (IOException e) {
    e.printStackTrace();
}
```

The last two `Files` methods allow a file to be parsed into lines of text; they conveniently wrap the `BufferedReader` method. Since creating a `BufferedReader` requires a `Charset` to manage byte-to-character conversion, the new `Files.lines` methods must be given a `Charset` also:

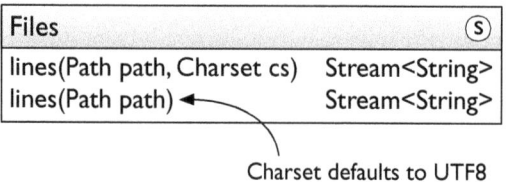

Charset defaults to UTF8

Naturally, `Files.lines` has similar performance characteristics as its underlying `BufferedReader` implementation.

java.util.regex.Pattern This class has always had a convenience method `split`, returning an array; in Java 8 it has added an analogous stream-bearing method `splitAsStream`:

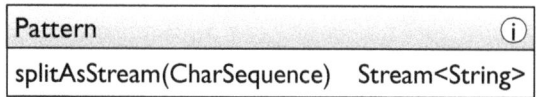

Like `split`, this method divides its input into substrings, each of which is terminated either by a subsequence matching this pattern or by the end of the input. Here are some examples to show the effect of different pattern matches at the beginning of

the input string. The method `exampleSplit` returns a string showing the splits made
by the supplied pattern on sample output from `ls -l`:

```
String exampleSplit(String pattern) {
    Pattern p = Pattern.compile(pattern);
    String s = "-rw-rw-r--  1 root admin  21508 26 Feb  2014 /.bashrc";
    return p.splitAsStream(s)
        .collect(joining("\",\"", "\"", "\""));
}
```

If the pattern does not match any subsequence of the input, then the resulting
stream contains a single element corresponding to the input sequence (line 2 of
Table 5-1). A match of non-zero width at the beginning of the input sequence results
in the insertion of an empty string at the beginning of the stream (line 3). A match of
zero width does not (line 4).

Input	Output
`"o+"`	`"-rw-rw-r-- 1 r","t admin 21508 26 Feb 2013 /.bashrc"`
`"@"`	`"-rw-rw-r-- 1 root admin 21508 26 Feb 2013 /.bashrc"`
`"^-"`	`"","rw-rw-r-- 1 root admin 21508 26 Feb 2013 /.bashrc"`
`"^"`	`"-rw-rw-r-- 1 root admin 21508 26 Feb 2013 /.bashrc"`

TABLE 5-1. *Behavior of* `exampleSplit`

`java.util.jar.JarFile`   Until now, entries in a jar file could be read in bulk only
via an `InputStream` or an `Enumeration`; a more convenient stream-bearing method
has now been added:

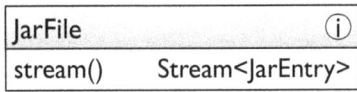

`java.util.zip.ZipFile`   The new method added to this class is similar to that for
`JarFile`:

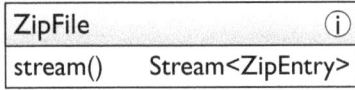

java.lang.CharSequence   Implementations of this interface include `String`, `StringBuffer`, `StringBuilder`, and `java.nio.CharBuffer`. Java 8 has added two stream-bearing methods, `chars` and `codePoints`, which behave identically for the most frequently used Unicode characters:

CharSequence	ⓘ
chars()	IntStream
codePoints()	IntStream

The difference between these two methods is in their handling of Unicode *supplementary characters*, that is, those whose code point is greater than U+FFFF. Supplementary characters include ideographs from East Asian languages and pictorial characters (including emojis). The method `chars` is generally preferable to `codePoints` on grounds of efficiency but, unlike `codePoints`, it does not interpret supplementary characters correctly.

The new methods return `IntStream` (the most appropriate choice in the absence of a primitive specialized `CharStream`), so it is useful to know how to convert the `int` values into a `Stream<Character>` if the need arises. The key point is that since boxing is required, `Stream.mapToObj` must be given the right primitive type to work on:

```
Stream<Character> chrStream = "example".chars().mapToObj(i -> (char)i);
```

java.util.BitSet   The `toString` method of this class has always returned a string representation of the set of indices of the bits that are set. Now the `stream` method returns these indices in a form ready for processing:

BitSet	ⓘ
stream()	IntStream

For example:

```
byte[] bits = {10, 18};              // 01010000 01001000 (little-endian)
BitSet bs = BitSet.valueOf(bits);
System.out.println(bs.stream()
    .boxed().collect(toList()));     // prints [1, 3, 9, 12]
```

java.util.Random and java.util.SplittableRandom   The four `Random` classes (`Random` has two subclasses, `SecureRandom` and `ThreadLocalRandom`) all expose the same methods for generating random streams. These methods are in three groups, corresponding to the primitive stream types that they return:

Random, SplittableRandom	ⓘ
ints()	IntStream
ints(int, int)	IntStream
ints(long)	IntStream
ints(long, int, int)	IntStream
longs()	LongStream
longs(long, long)	LongStream
longs(long)	LongStream
longs(long, long, long)	LongStream
doubles()	DoubleStream
doubles(double, double)	DoubleStream
doubles(long)	DoubleStream
doubles(long, double, double)	DoubleStream

Each group has four methods, providing different combinations of choice as to whether they deliver a fixed or unlimited number of values and whether each value delivered lies within a defined range. The class `SplittableRandom` was introduced in Java 8 to support parallel distribution of random number production. It is typically used in a `Spliterator` (an object used to create a stream, covered in detail later in this chapter) that, given the requirement to create a random series, will divide the series into segments, assigning a separate generator for the creation of each segment. The division uses the method `SplittableRandom.split`, which constructs and returns a new instance that shares no mutable state with this instance, but creates a series of values with the same statistical properties as the original.

Although the preceding list includes all the important stream-bearing methods in the platform library—in practice, the most commonly used stream sources—it is by no means the whole story: later in this chapter we shall see how defining a `Spliterator` enables you to create your own stream from any data source.

5.2 Spliterators and Fork/Join

This section continues our study of stream sources with a brief investigation of how they work. You can use streams effectively without understanding how they are created, as the examples in earlier chapters have shown. But you may want to know how the mechanics of stream creation influence performance—we will see the effects in Chapter 6—and further, understanding stream creation now will be useful later if you want to create your own streams from a source other than the platform classes. The worked example in the next section shows a small but realistic example.

Our starting point is the parallel divide-and-conquer algorithm that introduced streams in Chapter 1 (p. 12) and its implementation by the fork/join framework. The key class in the generation of parallel streams by the framework is a subclass of

ForkJoinTask; an instance of this class wraps a stream processing task, consisting of the data to be processed and the processing action to be applied to each element of that data. Task execution takes one of two alternative routes: either the data is processed iteratively in the calling thread, or it is divided, with a new task being created to process part of it on a different thread allocated from the ForkJoinPool, and the rest being assigned to the existing task, to be executed again in the calling thread.

So the data accessor that the task uses must support these two alternatives: splitting and iterative direct execution. The type of this data accessor is named for these two functions: java.util.Spliterator. The two key methods of a Spliterator correspond to its two key functions: trySplit, which causes it to divide itself, partitioning its data between itself and a new Spliterator, which it returns, and tryAdvance, which accepts a Consumer and applies it to the next element. Before looking more closely at Spliterator, let's first see how it works together with the fork/join framework.

The following pseudocode is an extreme simplification of the fork/join task described earlier. In this code, T is the type of the elements to be processed by the stream; the method makeAbstractTask creates a new task, setting its spliterator field. The value sizeThreshold has been calculated by the framework as the lowest task data size that is worth parallelizing, taking into account both the total original data size and the processing environment:

```
Spliterator<T> newSpliterator;
while (this.spliterator.estimateSize() > sizeThreshold &&
    (newSpliterator = this.spliterator.trySplit()) != null) {

    // the f/j framework and the spliterator have both agreed to a
    // split, and the spliterator's data has been divided between the
    // the new spliterator and itself; now wrap a new task around
    // the part of the data assigned to the new spliterator and
    // assign it for execution in another thread.

    makeTask(newSpliterator).fork();
}
// process remaining data by iteratively calling
// this.spliterator.tryAdvance() in this thread
```

The loop condition for this code shows that a decision to split rather than to process iteratively requires two criteria to be met:

- That a newly forked task could take advantage of currently unused processing capacity. In Java 8, the value of sizeThreshold is just the result of dividing the total data size by the number of threads available, but more sophisticated criteria might be used in the future by the framework to decide this.

- That the data structure's own conditions are met for making splitting worthwhile. A `Spliterator` is permitted to respond to a call of `trySplit` by returning `null` instead of a new `Spliterator`, perhaps because the data set is small enough that the gains from going parallel would not outweigh the overhead of splitting, or for some other reason.

These are the key methods of the `Spliterator` interface:

Spliterator<T>	ⓘ
trySplit()	Spliterator<T>
tryAdvance(Consumer<T>)	boolean
forEachRemaining(Consumer<T>)	void
estimateSize()	long
characteristics()	int

All except for `forEachRemaining` are abstract. A brief explanation of these methods follows. Development of a custom spliterator as part of the worked example in §5.4 should help to clarify further how spliterators work and when you would choose to write your own.

trySplit As we have seen, this method creates a new `Spliterator` and transfers some—ideally, half—of its elements to it. Splits that do not achieve this ideal may still be effective; for example, splitting an approximately balanced binary tree can still lead to useful parallelism. On the other hand we have `BufferedReader`, which cannot even approximate an equal split and, at an extreme, classes that cannot split at all and whose spliterators always decline to split (which is why the method `Collection.parallelStream` is specified to return a "possibly parallel" stream).

If order is significant for a stream source, then the elements that the spliterator covers after it has executed `trySplit` must succeed those covered by the spliterator that it returned.

tryAdvance This method combines the functions of the `Iterator` methods `next` and `hasNext`. If no elements remain, `tryAdvance` returns `false`; otherwise, it returns `true` after calling the `accept` method of the supplied `Consumer` with the next element as the argument. This is the heart of two of the major improvements that spliterators offer over iterators: fewer method calls are needed for each element, resulting in big performance improvements, and there is now no risk of the race conditions that can arise as a result of a collection being mutated between a call of `hasNext` and a call of `next`.

forEachRemaining Provides a bulk traversal mechanism: rather than returning after processing a single element, as `tryAdvance` does, this method processes all the remaining elements in the spliterator in a single call. This may provide performance improvements by eliminating the per-call overheads of `tryAdvance`. The default implementation simply calls `tryAdvance` repeatedly until it returns `false`.

estimateSize Returns an estimate of the number of elements covered by the spliterator. If the spliterator is supplying an infinite stream or if it would be too expensive to compute the size, `estimateSize` can return `Long.MAX_VALUE`. However, even an inexact estimate is often useful and inexpensive to compute.

characteristics Returns a set of characteristics (§6.3) for this spliterator.

5.2.1 Streams from Spliterators

Spliterators supply the essence of what is needed to make streams. To actually make them, the utility class `StreamSupport` provides methods that accept a `Spliterator` to create a reference stream, or one of `Spliterator`'s specialized primitive subtypes, `Spliterator.ofInt`, `Spliterator.ofLong`, or `Spliterator.ofDouble`, to create a primitive stream. In the last section of this chapter we will see a practical example of the creation of a stream from a custom spliterator.

It is worth noting here, however, that `StreamSupport.stream` can also be used as a slightly clumsier substitute for the stream-bearing methods of the `Collection` interface. That is because every `Collection` instance is an implementation of `Iterable`, which exposes a method `spliterator`. So for any `Iterable<T>`, iter say, you can write

```
Stream<T> str = StreamSupport.stream(iter.spliterator(), false);
```

where the argument `false` means that in this case the generated stream will be sequential rather than parallel. This is in fact how the stream-bearing methods of `Collection` are implemented.

The default implementation of `Iterable.spliterator` has poor performance, because any good splitting strategy will depend on the physical structure of the specific `Iterable`. So implementations will usually override it, as the classes of the Java Collections Framework do. But if you have to use an API that accepts or returns `Iterable` rather than `Collection` instances, it is worthwhile knowing this way of performing stream processing directly on them, rather than having to first dump them into a collection.

5.3 Exceptions

We saw in §2.7.2 that lambdas have no special mechanism for managing checked exceptions; any checked exception that a lambda throws must be explicitly declared by its function type. As a result, checked exceptions do not fit well with lazy evaluation as implemented in the Stream API. In this section we will explore the problems; it should also become clear why this section is located in the chapter on creating streams: the most common occurrence of checked exceptions in stream processing is in the API for files used as stream sources.

To disentangle the issues, we will look at a series of increasingly complex scenarios. The basic use case that we are working toward is the problem of listing the contents of every text file in a directory. The idea is that `Files.list` (p. 115), supplied with a directory path, generates a stream of file paths, one for each file in the directory; these are in turn supplied to `Files.lines`, which generates a stream of lines from each one. These streams can be concatenated into a single stream by `flatMap`. If no exceptions were in the picture, we could write, for any directory path `start`:

```
Files.list(start)
   .flatMap(Files::lines)
   .forEachOrdered(System.out::println);
```

This is the basis of the worked example later in this chapter (§5.4): an implementation in Java of `grep`, the Unix utility that matches lines in text files against regular expression patterns.

Since the problem revolves around the point at which exceptions are thrown, let's start with the basic case in which exception throwing is not delayed at all. The following code creates a stream of `Path` objects corresponding to the contents of the directory whose path is `start`. For the sake of the example, we will just create a stream without using it, and exception handling will be delegated to the caller by rethrowing the checked exception wrapped in the `RuntimeException` subclass `UncheckedIOException`. First, though, we will print a stack trace to show what has happened:

```
try (Stream<Path> paths = Files.list(start)) {          // line 19
} catch (IOException e) {
    e.printStackTrace();
    throw new UncheckedIOException(e);
}
```

`IOException` will be thrown and caught if `start` is not a path to a directory that can be opened for reading. For example, if the directory permissions make it inaccessible, the stack trace will look like this:

```
java.nio.file.AccessDeniedException: ./fooDir
    <omitted: frames for platform-specific filesystem access methods>
    at java.nio.file.Files.newDirectoryStream(Files.java:457)
    at java.nio.file.Files.list(Files.java:3448)
    at ExceptionsExample.main(ExceptionsExample.java:19)
```

This is in line with our ideas of how exceptions normally work, though perhaps not obviously in line with our expectations about the lazy evaluation of streams. No terminal method has been invoked on the stream created by the call of `Files.list`, so its elements have not been evaluated. But the attempt to open the directory `./fooDir` has been made eagerly.

Next, suppose instead that the directory has been opened and the stream of paths has been constructed successfully. Now `flatMap` calls `Files.lines`, which will first open each file and then read its contents into a stream of lines that will be appended into the stream to be returned. What will happen if the attempt to open one of these files fails? As the introduction to `Files` mentioned (p. 115), I/O-based stream-creating methods like `Files.lines` throw the checked exception `IOException` in this situation. Instead of a directory, we can make a file inaccessible to show the problem; in the interests of having the simplest possible intermediate operation, we use `peek` to evaluate the behavioral parameter:

```
try (Stream<Path> paths = Files.list(start)) {
    paths.peek(path -> {
        try {
            Files.lines(path);                      // line 42
        } catch (IOException e) {
            System.err.println("** exception from Files.lines");
            e.printStackTrace();
        }
    })
    .forEach(line -> {});                           // line 47
} catch (IOException e) {
    System.err.println("++ exception from Files.list");
    e.printStackTrace();
    throw new UncheckedIOException(e);
}
```

That code produces the following output:

```
** exception from Files.lines
java.nio.file.AccessDeniedException: ./fooDir/barFile
    <omitted: frames for filesystem access methods>
    at java.nio.file.Files.lines(Files.java:3782)
    at ExceptionsExample.lambda$main$0(ExceptionsExample.java:42)
    at ExceptionsExample$$Lambda$2/1149319664.accept(Unknown Source)
```

```
<omitted: frames for stream implementation methods>
at java.util.stream.ReferencePipeline.forEach(↵
                                  ReferencePipeline.java:418)
at ExceptionsExample.main(ExceptionsExample.java:47)
```

Notice the stack frame for `forEach`. This corresponds with our understanding that it is execution of the terminal operation that initiates evaluation of the pipeline elements.

Finally, we can replace the call of `peek` with `flatMap`, which will take the streams of strings from each file and concatenate them into a single stream:

```
try (Stream<Path> paths = Files.list(start)) {
    paths.flatMap(path -> {
        Stream<String> lines;
        try {
            lines = Files.lines(path);
        } catch (IOException e) {
            e.printStackTrace();
            lines = Stream.of("Unreadable file: " + path);
        }
        return lines;
    })
    .forEach(line -> {});          // line 57
} catch (IOException e) {
    e.printStackTrace();
    throw new UncheckedIOException(e);
}
```

In this version, the failure to open a file will produce a stack trace very like the last example. But suppose instead that `Files.lines` succeeds in opening a file and returns a stream, as yet unevaluated, of the lines that it contains. Once the files are open, the terminal operation will call the flattening code to concatenate the separate streams of lines into a single stream. In order to do this, the streams must be evaluated and the now-opened files must be read; this action too can fail. But the lambda whose execution opened the file is now out of scope and the file-reading code is being called directly, so failure notification must take place via an unchecked exception. To emphasize this, we can break the pipeline code down to an equivalent version in which each stage is extracted to a local variable:

```
Stream<Path> paths = Files.list(start);
Stream<String> lines = paths.flatMap(path -> ...);
lines.forEach(line -> {});
```

Since `flatMap` is no longer on the call stack when its lambda fails, its `throws` clause is irrelevant. For this reason, platform library code used to create streams always wraps checked exceptions in unchecked ones. The most common cases are covered by wrapping `IOException` in the new `java.io.UncheckedIOException`; this is thrown when failures occur after a file has been opened. In the case of such a failure, the stack trace will look like this:

```
Exception in thread "main" java.io.UncheckedIOException:↵
               java.nio.charset.MalformedInputException: Input length = 1
   at java.io.BufferedReader$1.hasNext(BufferedReader.java:574)
   <omitted: frames corresponding to stream implementation methods>
   at java.util.stream.ReferencePipeline.forEach(↵
                                      ReferencePipeline.java:418)
   at ExceptionsExample.main(ExceptionsExample.java:57)
Caused by: java.nio.charset.MalformedInputException: Input length = 1
   at java.nio.charset.CoderResult.throwException(CoderResult.java:281)
   <omitted: frames for text file reading and charset decoding>
   at java.io.BufferedReader$1.hasNext(BufferedReader.java:571)
   ... 18 more
```

This stack results from the evaluation of one of the streams of lines raising a `MalformedInputException`, thrown in the course of processing a file by a `Charset` that has encountered a Unicode character it cannot decode (for example, as a result of attempting to read a binary file as though it were text). This checked exception is caught by the `hasNext` method of `BufferedReader` (called from `Files.lines`) and wrapped in an `UncheckedIOException` that rises uncaught to the top of the call stack. The "18 more" stack frames referred to at the bottom of the checked exception stack are the same 18 frames that constitute the whole of the unchecked stack above it; the duplication is omitted for brevity.

So lazily evaluated code called from within pipeline operations can throw only unchecked exceptions, which will end the terminal operation and so stop pipeline processing altogether. If instead we expect errors from which we want to recover, they must be notified by checked exceptions thrown from eagerly evaluated operations. For example, we saw earlier that attempting to read characters from a binary file results in a (checked) `MalformedInputException`; for the current use case—printing the contents of every text file in a directory—there is a simple recovery action: skip that file. But that can only be taken if the method throwing it is eagerly evaluated, as happens with `Files.readAllLines`, which eagerly reads an entire file, throwing a checked exception if it encounters an undecodable byte sequence. It is this method that will form the basis of our solution to the recursive `grep` problem of the next section.

5.4 Worked Example: Recursive grep

The command-line utility `grep` was originally written as a stand-alone application for an early version of Unix, to search text files for lines matching a supplied pattern in the form of a regular expression and, by default, to print them. Since then, `grep`, in different variants, has become standard in the core library of every version of Unix and Linux. Various options can modify its actions in different ways, including:

- Recursively searching entire directory subtrees

- Searching for lines that do *not* match the pattern

- Suppression of match printing

- Printing the names of files containing matches (instead of, or as well as, printing the matching lines)

- Printing the count of matches in each file searched

- Printing the context of a match (several lines before or after the match)

The exercise of reproducing the behavior of `grep` using streams is interesting in itself, and potentially useful for embedding `grep`'s functionality within a Java program. (But please note: if you really are thinking of creating a performant `grep` substitute, you should pay close attention to the spliterator implementation at the end of this section.) We will begin by executing the simplest `grep` behavior on each file in a directory tree, and then go on to incorporate a few of its many options.

grep -Rh   The first version of the problem is to search every file whose name begins with `test` and has the extension `.txt`, anywhere in the filesystem under the directory `startDir`, for mixed decimal numbers. These will match with the regular expression "`[-+]?[0-9]*\.?[0-9]+`". Our program will imitate the behavior of `grep -Rh`: the `-R` option forces `grep` to search the filesystem recursively, and the `-h` option prevents the usual prefixing of each matching output line with the name of the file in which it was found. (Implementing that feature will be the next problem after this one.) We will need the following preliminary declarations:

```
Path start = new File("startDir").toPath();
Pattern pattern = Pattern.compile("[-+]?[0-9]*\.?[0-9]+");
PathMatcher pathMatcher =
            FileSystems.getDefault().getPathMatcher("**/test*.txt");
```

Two kinds of pattern matching are in use here: regular expressions and *globbing*, which you may know as shell pattern matching. Globbing is used here to show how easily it can be introduced into stream-processing programs. Although it is less powerful than regular expression matching, it is much more concise and convenient in those cases where it does work.

A suitable starting point is the code we developed in exploring the subject of exceptions thrown in pipeline operations (p. 123). Here it is repeated for convenience, only changed in respect of an added assumption that the enclosing method can rethrow an IOException resulting from a failure to open the start directory, so it need not be handled in this code:

```
try (Stream<Path> paths = Files.list(start)) {
    paths.flatMap(path -> {
        Stream<String> lines;
        try {
            lines = Files.lines(path);
        } catch (IOException e) {
            e.printStackTrace();
            lines = Stream.of("Unreadable file: " + a);
        }
        return lines;
    })
    .forEach(line -> {});
} // no longer catching IOException
```

This requires some alterations before it can become our first version. Stop reading for a moment, examine the code carefully, and make a list of the changes that are needed to make it satisfy the problem description given. (We will still leave calls of printStackTrace as placeholders for exception handling.)

––––––––––––––––––––––––––

Here is a list of the changes needed:

- Calling Files.list, we will see only files in startDir. To search a directory subtree, we should use Files.walk (see p. 115).

- For the reasons explored in the discussion of exceptions, the call of the lazily evaluated method Files.lines must be wrapped in code that rethrows IOException as UncheckedIOException, or replaced by a call to Files.readAllLines (p. 126). Files.readAllLines returns a list of strings that can be used as a stream source.

- The pipeline needs some filters on the paths produced by Files.walk: to remove directories from the Path stream (this is more efficient than letting them be trapped by a failure in readAllLines), and to ensure that only files matching the name pattern "**/test*.txt" are processed.

- Filters are also needed on the text lines returned from the files: to remove the empty strings resulting from processing of non-text files and, of course, to remove lines that do not match the regular expression.

- The terminal operation should print the matching lines. It uses `forEach`, which does not impose ordering, except accidentally. For the moment, let's diverge from `grep` by assuming that we only care about getting the matching lines, not about the order in which they appear.

Applying these changes to the preceding code, we get code that reproduces the behavior of `grep -h`:

```
try (Stream<Path> pathStream = Files.walk(start)) {
    pathStream
        .filter(Files::isRegularFile)
        .filter(pathMatcher::matches)
        .flatMap(path -> {
            try {
                return Files.readAllLines(path).stream();
            } catch (IOException e) {
                return Stream.of("");
            }
        })
        .filter(line -> ! line.isEmpty())
        .filter(line -> pattern.matcher(line).find())
        .forEach(System.out::println);
}
```

grep -R   For the first variant on this solution, consider removing the option -h so that `grep` is required to prefix every output line with the path of the file in which it was found. Before reading on, stop and think how you would change the preceding code to implement this, restructuring it if necessary.

_____

Clearly, the path can only be prefixed to the lines of the file at a point where it is still available, which means within the lambda for the `flatMap`. In the body of the inner `try`, the lambda parameter `path` is in scope and can be prefixed to each line:

```
try {
    return Files.readAllLines(path).stream()
        .map(line -> path + ": " + line);
} catch (IOException e) {
    return Stream.of("");
}
```

That is a solution, of sorts. But it's unsatisfactorily wasteful, in that it is performing string concatenation—an expensive operation—for every line in every text file, even though many of them are likely to be discarded by the regex matching filter later on. That can easily be avoided by moving the regex matching filter from its present downstream position to *before* the path is concatenated with each line:

```
try {
    return Files.readAllLines(path).stream()
        .filter(line -> pattern.matcher(line).find())
        .map(line -> path + ": " + line);
} catch (IOException e) {
    return Stream.of("");
}
```

And the solution to this problem is a small modification of the preceding one:

```
try (Stream<Path> pathStream = Files.walk(start)) {
    pathStream
        .filter(Files::isRegularFile)
        .filter(pathMatcher::matches)
        .flatMap(path -> {
            try {
                return Files.readAllLines(path).stream()
                    .filter(line -> pattern.matcher(line).find());
                    .map(line -> path + ": " + line);
            } catch (IOException e) {
                return Stream.of("");
            }
        })
        .filter(line -> ! line.isEmpty())
        .forEach(System.out::println);
}
```

grep -Rc The -c option suppresses normal output, instead printing a count of matching lines for each input file. Again, stop and think how to do this before reading on.

This solution is quite straightforward, once you see that since the output lines are one-to-one with files containing matching text, the output from each file must be collected into a single string before being passed to the terminal operation. So map rather than flatMap is the appropriate operation, with each path, startDir/foo say, being mapped to a string like "startDir/foo: 3". The line count can be obtained from the terminal operation `count` that applied a stream of matching lines for each file. This gives us:

```
try (Stream<Path> pathStream = Files.walk(start)) {
    pathStream
        .filter(Files::isRegularFile)
        .filter(pathMatcher::matches)
        .map(path -> {
            try {
                long matchCount = Files.readAllLines(path).stream()
                    .filter(line -> pattern.matcher(line).find())
                    .count();
                return matchCount == 0 ? "" : path + ": " + matchCount;
            } catch (IOException e) {
                return "";
            }
        })
        .filter(line -> ! line.isEmpty())
        .forEach(System.out::println);
}
```

grep -b   The -b option requires each line of output to be prefixed by its character displacement in the file. So a search for the pattern "`w.*t`" in this farsighted tribute to immutability:[1]

```
The Moving Finger writes; and, having writ,
Moves on: nor all thy Piety nor Wit
Shall lure it back to cancel half a Line,
Nor all thy Tears wash out a Word of it.
```

should produce the output

```
44:Moves on: nor all thy Piety nor Wit
122:Nor all thy Tears wash out a Word of it.
```

   At first sight, this looks very like the book displacement problem of Chapter 4 (p. 90), and indeed one option would be to solve it in just the same way using a custom collector. Closer examination, however, shows an important difference in grep -b that will lead to a better solution. The book displacement problem requires the calculation of a running total, making it an example of a *prefix sum*, a problem in which the value of every element depends on the values of the preceding ones. In a naïve parallel algorithm for prefix sum, like the book displacement example, the total cost of the combine operations (that is, the total delay imposed by them) is proportional to the

---

[1] *The Rubaiyyat of Omar Khayyam* (q. 51), trans. Edward Fitzgerald, 1st edition

size of the input data set, so going parallel may not produce the performance gains that we would like to see.[2]

The current problem can be recast, however, to avoid this difficulty. If we could treat the data of the input file as a byte array in memory, the displacement of each line could be determined without any need to use the displacements of its predecessors. The *memory mapping* feature of Java NIO provides exactly this ability; its use allows the operating system to manage the correspondence between filestore and memory transparently and efficiently. For medium or large files (memory mapping is usually worthwhile only for files of hundreds of kilobytes in size, or more), memory mapping can offer big performance gains; in particular, random access carries no performance penalty. Memory mapping is implemented in Java by the class `java.nio.MappedByteBuffer`.

Notice that the earlier `grep` examples, like most file processing tasks, are also unlikely to benefit from parallelization, because the performance bottleneck will be at the file input stage rather than in stream processing. So the `Spliterator` technique we are about to use would improve performance for any such task, provided that the file is large enough to justify the overhead of memory mapping.

In this problem, memory mapping has the added advantage of allowing us to avoid having to calculate the displacement of each line from that of its predecessor; instead, when the custom spliterator breaks the buffer into lines, the displacement of each line will be known from its index in the buffer. The function of the spliterator will be to supply the stream with value objects, each of which encapsulates a line together with its index:

```
class DispLine {
    final int disp;
    final String line;
    DispLine(int d, String l) { disp = d; line = l; }
    public String toString() { return disp + " " + line; }
}
```

Spliterators are usually named by the data structure that they are splitting, but to describe this spliterator adequately, its name should include not only its data structure, `ByteBuffer`, but also the type of the objects that it will yield. Since the name `ByteBufferToDispLineSpliterator` is too long to use in code to be printed in book form, we'll abbreviate it to `LineSpliterator`. A `LineSpliterator` is constructed to cover a range of the `ByteBuffer` bounded by two indices, `lo` and `hi`, both inclusive, supplied at construction time:

---

[2] The seriousness of this problem depends on how expensive the combine operation is. Java 8 provided `java.util.Arrays` with various overloads of a new method `parallelPrefix` for computing prefix sums efficiently, but this innovation has not yet reached the Stream API.

```
class LineSpliterator implements Spliterator<DispLine> {
    private ByteBuffer bb;
    private int lo, hi;
    LineSpliterator(ByteBuffer bb, int lo, int hi) {
        this.bb = bb; this.lo = lo; this.hi = hi;
    }
    // implementation of the abstract methods of Spliterator
}
```

Before reading on, see how much of the implementation of `LineSpliterator` you can supply, starting with `trySplit`.

Figure 5-1 shows the buffer at the start of processing. The range of the first spliterator created is the data in the entire buffer, including the terminating newline byte.

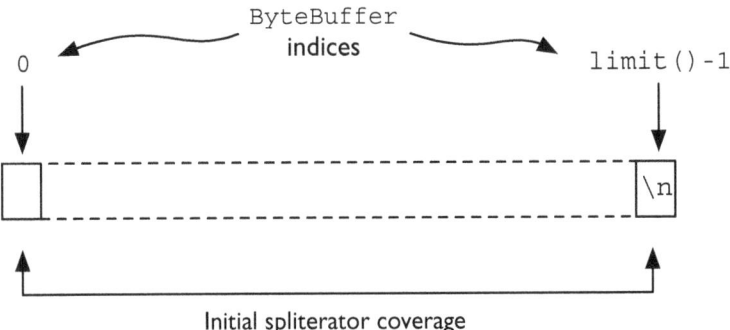

FIGURE 5-1.   *Initial `LineSpliterator` configuration*

If this range is to be split, the aim will be to divide the buffer into two approximately equal parts, each of them again terminated by a newline. A suitable dividing point between the parts will be found by making a linear search for a newline, in either direction, starting from the midpoint of the buffer. This search represents the algorithmic part of the overhead of splitting (the rest is the infrastructure overhead of creating and forking a new fork/join task). Its cost is proportional to the average line length, rather than to the total buffer size as with the book displacement program (§4.3.2).

Figure 5-2 shows this search process and the coverage of the two spliterators that result.

Suppose, however, that the search fails to detect a newline character before encountering the end of the `LineSpliterator` range. Given that it starts from the range

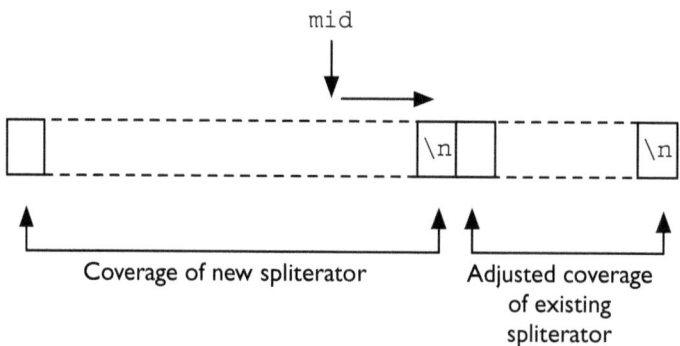

mid

Coverage of new spliterator

Adjusted coverage
of existing
spliterator

FIGURE 5-2. *Operation of LineSpliterator.trySplit*

midpoint, such a failure suggests that there are probably only a few lines in the entire range—possibly only one—so in this situation it is reasonable to decline to split by returning null rather than searching for a newline in the opposite direction.

Once you have understood the algorithm for trySplit, the code is straightforward:

```
public Spliterator<DispLine> trySplit() {
    int mid = (lo + hi) >>> 1;
    while (bb.get(index) != '\\n') mid++;
    LineSpliterator newSpliterator = null;
    if (mid != hi) {
        newSpliterator = new LineSpliterator(bb, lo, mid);
        lo = mid + 1;
    }
    return newSpliterator;
}
```

If you have not already written code for tryAdvance, stop now and sketch an implementation.

The purpose of tryAdvance is to facilitate processing of the next available DispLine instance. It searches for the next newline character, creates a DispLine instance from the bytes traversed in the search, and applies its supplied Consumer argument to it. Finally, it reduces the spliterator's range to exclude the bytes just processed, and returns a boolean signifying the availability of further input.

```
public boolean tryAdvance(Consumer<? super DispLine> action) {
    int index = lo;
    StringBuilder sb = new StringBuilder();
    do {
        sb.append((char)bb.get(index));
    } while (bb.get(index++) != '\\n');
    action.accept(new DispLine(lo, sb.toString()));
    lo = lo + sb.length();
    return lo <= hi;
}
```

Two other `Spliterator` methods must be overridden. The method `estimateSize` returns an estimate, necessarily approximate in this case, of the number of elements that would be returned by repeated calls of `tryAdvance`.

```
public long estimateSize() { return (hi - lo + 1)/AVERAGE_LINE-LENGTH; }
```

The method `characteristics` returns the characteristics of this `Spliterator`, used by the framework to choose appropriate optimizations (see §6.3). Here is a suitable implementation of `characteristics` for this problem:

```
public int characteristics() { return ORDERED | IMMUTABLE | NONNULL; }
```

Finally, here is how `LineSpliterator` could be used to simulate the action of `grep -b`. This is the code for searching a single file; the earlier examples show how it could be extended it to a recursive search:

```
try (FileChannel fc = FileChannel.open(start)) {
    MappedByteBuffer bB =
                fc.map(FileChannel.MapMode.READ_ONLY, 0, fc.size());
    Spliterator<DispLine> ls =
                new LineSpliterator(bB, 0, bB.limit() - 1);
    StreamSupport.stream(ls, true)
        .filter(dl -> pattern.matcher(dl.line).find())
        .forEachOrdered(System.out::print);
}
```

We saw `StreamSupport` used earlier (§5.2.1) to create streams from spliterators. In this case, we are supplying `true` as the second parameter to `StreamSupport.stream` to ensure that a parallel, rather than sequential, stream will be generated. For the terminal operation, we are using `forEachOrdered` to produce the output. This is in contrast to the earlier examples in which, as we saw, there is little point in invoking parallelism. In principle, of course, out-of-order execution is possible with `forEach` even on sequential streams, but that might have been acceptable for the earlier `grep` options. For this one, however, a user would certainly be surprised if the matching lines appeared in a random order.

Summarizing this section, we should note that programming a `grep` equivalent has shown some strengths of the Stream API: the solutions for the earlier examples are straightforward, and respecifying the problem to simulate the different options required only small corresponding changes in the code. In the last example, we saw how cooperation with Java NIO enables the Stream API to process input from large files with, as we shall see in §6.7, a very high degree of parallel speedup.

5.5 Conclusion

This chapter had three connected purposes: to explore the library facilities for creating streams, to explain the mechanism by which stream creation works, and to show how and why you would write your own implementation of it. We saw that stream-bearing methods have been added to a wide variety of platform classes, allowing streams to fulfill their role of conveying any kind of data for processing through intermediate operations and into a terminal operation. In processing streams from any of these methods, you gain the advantages in expressiveness and readability of parallel-ready code; whether you can effectively extract parallelism depends, as we have seen, on how effectively the stream source can split its data. Splittability is only part of the story, however; in Chapter 6 we will see how it combines with other factors, such as data set size and pipeline workload, to determine the overall speedup that can be obtained by parallelization.

The main example of the chapter showed off some of the strengths of the Stream API: the solutions for the earlier `grep` options were straightforward, and respecifying the problem to simulate the different options required only small corresponding changes in the code. In the last part of the example, we saw how cooperation with Java NIO enables the Stream API to process input from large files with, as we shall see in §6.7, a very high degree of parallel speedup.

CHAPTER
6

Stream Performance

T his book has put forward two reasons for using lambdas and streams: to get better programs, and to get better performance. By now, the code examples should have demonstrated the claim for better programs, but we have not yet examined the claims about performance. In this chapter, those claims will be investigated through the technique of microbenchmarking.

This is a dangerous business: results from microbenchmarking run the risk of being used to guide program design in unsuitable situations. Since the overwhelming majority of situations are unsuitable, that is a serious problem! For example, a programmer's intuition is a highly unreliable guide for locating performance bottlenecks in a complex system; the only sure way to find them is to measure program behavior. So initial development, in which there is no working system to measure, is a prime instance of an unsuitable time for applying optimizations.

This is important, because mistakenly optimizing code that is not performance-critical is actually harmful.

- It wastes valuable effort, since even successful optimization will not improve overall system performance.

- It diverts attention from the important objectives of program design—to produce code that is well structured, readable, and maintainable.

- Source-code optimizations may well prevent just-in-time compilers from applying their own (current and future) optimizations, because these optimizations are tuned to work on common idioms.

That said, programmers enjoy learning about code performance, and there are real benefits to doing so. Foremost among these is the ability provided to developers by the Stream API to tune code—by choosing between sequential and parallel execution—without altering its design or behavior. This kind of unobtrusive performance management is new to the Java core libraries, but may become as successful and widespread here as it already is in enterprise programming. To take advantage of it, you need a mental model of the influences on the performance of streams.

However, even if you never act on that model directly, it can help to guide (but not dictate!) your design, complementing the mental model that programmers already have for the execution of traditional Java code.[1] In addition, the situations do exist in which optimization really is justified. Suppose, for a simple example, that you have identified a performance-critical bulk processing step and you now want to decide between the options for implementing it. Should you use a loop or a stream? If you use a stream, you often have a choice of different combinations of intermediate op-

---

[1] Unfortunately, the commonplace mental model for performance is itself sadly out of date; many programmers are unaware of JIT optimizations or the effect of hardware features like pipelining and multicore CPUs.

erations and collectors; which will perform best? This chapter will present results like Figure 6-1 to help answer such questions:

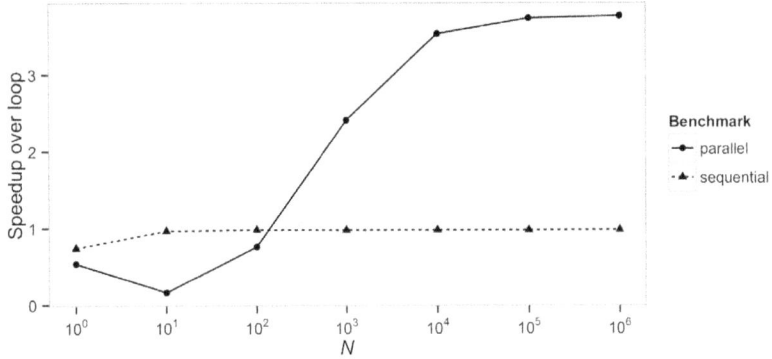

FIGURE 6-1. *Stream performance: sequential and parallel streams*

Figure 6-1 might be an interesting and useful result, but we need to know more. As it stands, it provides no information about the experimental conditions under which its result was obtained. The results will have been influenced both by factors external to the benchmark—varying system load, the behavior of other processes, network and disk activity, the hardware, operating system, and JVM configurations—and by properties of the benchmark itself: the data being processed and the operations that were performed.

Obviously, this is a problem; we want to be able to discuss performance of stream operations without taking all these factors into consideration. How can we get meaningful results from highly simplified observations of such complex systems? To draw an analogy—only a little far-fetched—think of the difficulty of trialing a new drug on humans. The goal of a trial might be simple—to discover if a drug is effective in treating a certain disease—but achieving it isn't simple at all: you can't just administer the drug to a person with the disease and observe whether they are cured. Many factors can influence the result: the background health of the subject, their diet, age, gender, and often many others. All of these factors can affect the result for any individual.

Of course, working computer systems are not nearly so complex as biological systems, but they are complex enough for observational experiments to share the problem: just as you can't draw a conclusion about a drug's effectiveness by simply administering it to someone and observing the outcome, you can't change a line of code in a working system and expect to get a useful result simply by observing the outcome. In both cases there are too many variables involved. In the next section we will look at an experimental method for eliminating these effects as far as we can. Then, in the rest of the chapter, we'll apply that method to measuring performance of stream operations.

Many of the experiments in this chapter are derived from examples used earlier for explaining stream programming techniques. These examples almost all illustrate the use of reference streams; for this reason, and because in practice it is reference streams that will raise the important performance questions, it is these rather than primitive streams that are the main focus of this chapter.

6.1 Microbenchmarking

Our aim is to discover the execution cost of a particular code fragment. But the argument in this chapter so far has been that a measurement of that cost is meaningful only in a working system under realistic load. Profiling or metering a production system is often not practicable; the alternative, of simulating the production system on a load-testing platform, is more feasible but still involves the difficulty of setting up an environment that reproduces the production system in all aspects: hardware and operating system configuration, demand on resources by other processes, the network and disk environments, and of course simulated typical and extreme loads.

A more practicable alternative is *microbenchmarking*, which *compares* two different code fragments operating in an isolated (and unrealistic) system. Each of these results will be meaningless in absolute terms, but the comparison between them can be meaningful—provided all those aspects are *controlled*. The idea of a controlled experiment is simple in principle. If all the factors listed earlier (the hardware and software environments, the system load, and so on) are held constant and only the code being compared is allowed to vary, then variation in the results must be due to what has been changed.

6.1.1 Measuring a Dynamic Runtime

Even when we have succeeded in controlling external influences on program behavior, other pitfalls await. Suppose our experiment follows this common template:

```
long start = System.currentTimeMillis();
// execute code being benchmarked
long end = System.currentTimeMillis();
System.out.println("My task executed in " + (end - start) + " ms.");
```

The apparent simplicity of this pattern hides some serious difficulties. Some of these relate to the measuring process itself, particularly for short run times: System.currentTimeMillis may be much less accurate than its name suggests, because it depends on a system clock that on some platforms may be updated only every 15ms or less. A better alternative on many platforms may be `System.nanoTime`, whose update resolution is typically only microseconds (but which can add significant measurement overhead). Further, these system calls measure elapsed time, so they include overheads like garbage collection.

The JVM itself also contributes misleading effects. Many of these relate to the dozens of optimizations that are applied by the bytecode-to-native compiler. Here are just three examples of the type of measurement problems that JVM operation can produce.

Warmup effects Measuring the cost of performing, say, the first 100 executions of a code fragment will often produce quite different results from taking the same measurement a minute later. A variety of initialization overheads may contribute to the earlier measurement, for example class loading—an expensive operation, which the JVM delays until the classes concerned are actually required. Another potent source of inaccuracies is provided by JIT compilation: initially the JVM interprets bytecode directly, but compiles it to native code when it has been executed enough times to qualify as a "hot spot" (and then continues to profile it in the interests of possible further optimization). The compilation overhead, followed by markedly improved performance, will give results far out of line with the steady-state observations that we require.

Dead code elimination A recurrent problem in writing microbenchmarks is ensuring that something is done with the result of the computation. Dead code elimination (DCE), an important compiler optimization, has the purpose of eliminating code that has no effect. For example, the following code is a naïve attempt to measure the cost of addition:

```
long start = System.currentTimeMillis();
long sum = 0;
for (int i = 0 ; i < 1_000_000 ; i++) {
    sum += i;
}
long end = System.currentTimeMillis();
System.out.println("Elapsed time: " + (end - start) + "ms");
```

Running this test on a modern JVM will result in very low execution times, because the compiler can detect that since `sum` is never used, it is unnecessary to calculate it and therefore unnecessary to execute the loop at all. In this case, there is a simple remedy: including the final value of `sum` in the output statement should ensure that it has to be calculated, although even then a compiler may detect that it can use an algebraic formula to calculate it without iterating; in general it is quite difficult to devise ways of preventing the compiler from applying DCE without distorting the measurements by introducing expensive new operations.

Garbage collection This is not a result of optimizations, but is a problem inherent in measuring programs that use automatic memory management: almost all benchmarks create objects, and some of these will become garbage while the benchmark is running. Eventually the garbage collector will be called, and its execution will contribute to the timing results. It may be possible to reduce this effect by manually triggering garbage collection before a measurement, but this might be unrealistic: in fact, it may be desirable to include garbage collection effects in the benchmark measurements if they will have a significant impact on performance in production. A better possibility may be to run the programs long enough for these costs to be amortized over many iterations.

6.1.2 The Java Microbenchmarking Harness

These effects, and many others, must be controlled to ensure that we have measured what we wanted to. Controlling them is such a common—and difficult—problem that benchmarking frameworks have become popular. These frameworks create custom test classes specifically designed to avoid the numerous pitfalls of microbenchmarking. The test classes are synthesized by the framework from benchmarking source code that you supply. Examples of benchmarking frameworks are Google Caliper (http://code.google.com/p/caliper) and the framework used to obtain the results of this chapter, the Java Microbenchmarking Harness (JMH) (http://openjdk.java.net/projects/code-tools/jmh).

JMH helps to solve the problems listed in the previous section. For example, the JMH API includes a static method, `Blackhole.consumeCPU`, which consumes CPU time in proportion to its argument without side-effect and without risking DCE and other optimizations. (The absolute amount of time used is unimportant, because `consumeCPU` will only ever be used for comparisons between microbenchmarks.)

To create a benchmark using JMH, you only have to annotate a method with `@Benchmark`. JMH has different modes of use; in the throughput mode, it executes each annotated method repeatedly for a time period you specify, automatically passing the returned value to the method `Blackhole.consume` to avoid DCE. For example, here is one of the three methods used to generate the graph at the beginning of this chapter. In this case the returned value will always be an empty `Optional`, but the requirement to return it means that the VM must evaluate the filter predicate for every stream element:

```
@Benchmark
public Optional<Integer> sequential()  {
    return integerList.stream()
        .filter(l -> { Blackhole.consumeCPU(payload); return false; })
        .findFirst();
}
```

6.1.3 Experimental Method

Finally, we apply two of the standard safeguards of experimental science to the results of our experiments.

Statistics   Given the number of factors that we now know affect microbenchmarking measurements, we can hardly expect that the same experiment, repeated several times, will produce exactly the same result; the influence of different external factors will vary from one set of observations to another. We can calculate a point estimate (such as the mean) for the most probable value, but that will have little meaning if external factors dominate the experiments. If we can assume that the effects of external factors are varying randomly, then running the same experiment a number of times can increase our confidence in the result. This can be quantified in a *confidence interval* (CI)—a range of values within which we can state with a degree of certainty (conventionally 95%) that the "true" value lies—that is, the value that we might get from many experiments. The larger the experiment, the narrower the confidence intervals that we can obtain.

Confidence intervals give us a useful indicator of experimental significance: if CIs from two different situations do not overlap, it is an indication that these situations really do give different results, always assuming that the other factors are varying randomly in a way that would not bias one set compared to another. In practice, for the experiments of this chapter, the variation between conditions is small compared to the differences in the means, and the number of trials is large enough that the confidence intervals are in practice too small to appear on the plots.

Open peer review   Like all scientific experiments, performance measurements are subject to flaws and bias. A partial safeguard against these sources of error is to enable open peer review of measurement experiments. This means publishing not only the summarized results, but also enough detail about the experimental conditions to enable others to reproduce and check them. This information includes the hardware, operating system, and JVM environments, as well as statistical information about the results. What follows is an example: a benchmark and its resulting data as used for Figure 6-1. Instead of tediously reproducing this information for each experiment in this chapter, a URL refers to the location on the book website of the full setup; as the experiments are easy to reproduce, raw experimental results are not usually provided.

```
@State(Scope.Benchmark) // The objects of this scope (e.g., instance
                        // variables) are shared between all threads.

public class CompareByN {

    // entire benchmark is run for each value of the @Param annotation
    @Param({"1", "10", "100", "1000", "10000", "100000", "1000000"})
```

```
    public int N;

    private final int payload = 50;
    private List<Integer> integerList;

    @Setup(Level.Trial)
    public void setUp() {
        integerList = IntStream.range(0, N).boxed().collect(toList());
    }

    @Benchmark
    public void iterative(Blackhole bh) {
        for (Integer i : integerList) {
            Blackhole.consumeCPU(payload);
            bh.consume(i);
        }
    }

    @Benchmark
    public Optional<Integer> sequential() {
        return integerList.stream()
            .filter(l -> {
                Blackhole.consumeCPU(payload);
                return false;
            })
            .findFirst();
    }

    @Benchmark
    public Optional<Integer> parallel() {
        return integerList.stream().parallel()
            .filter(l -> {
                Blackhole.consumeCPU(payload);
                return false;
            })
            .findFirst();
    }
}
```

JMH was used to run these benchmarks with their default settings—for each value of limit, it starts a new JVM, then performs the following sequence (called an "iteration") for each of the annotated methods:

1. For the warmup, it executes the method repeatedly for one second, 20 times over.

2. For the measurement, it again executes the method repeatedly for one second, 20 times over; this time, it records the number of times the method could be called in each one-second run (the "Score").

Each line in Table 6-1 shows, for a given data set size, the mean execution count and the confidence interval for a sample of 20 iterations.

This table shows the results, somewhat simplified, of executing the benchmark above on JDK1.8u5, running Linux (kernel version 3.11.0) on an Intel Core 2 Q8400 Quad CPU (2.66 GHz) with 2MB L2 cache. The column headed "Error (99.9%)" shows the spread of values in the 99.9 percent confidence interval (99.9% is the JMH default CI, very demanding by normal statistical standards).

Benchmark	Param:N	Score	Score Error (99.9%)
CompareByN.iterative	1	435668.6	429.0
	10	43001.1	2.9
	100	4316.4	175.8
	1000	432.3	0.1
	10000	43.2	0.2
	100000	4.3	0.0
	1000000	0.4	0.0
CompareByN.parallel	1	390068.6	769.7
	10	33339.6	406.2
	100	10674.4	128.5
	1000	1556.4	8.2
	10000	168.1	1.2
	100000	16.8	0.4
	1000000	1.6	0.0
CompareByN.sequential	1	412777.1	1053.1
	10	42967.8	6.3
	100	4286.6	8.9
	1000	428.0	3.7
	10000	43.6	0.0
	100000	4.3	0.0
	1000000	0.4	0.0

TABLE 6-1. *Sample Results for the Benchmark of Figure 6-3*

The rest of this chapter will present microbenchmarking results in the form of graphs like Figure 6-1 without providing this level of detail. But it is important that you know everything should be available: the full conditions for each experiment, the statistical methods used to prepare the presentation, and, where necessary, the raw results. This should give you confidence that you can review the method of the experiment, if necessary repeat it for yourself, and—most importantly—design and execute your own measurement experiments.

You should read what follows with a warning in mind: developments in hardware and in the Java platform will sooner or later change many of the trade-offs discussed here, generally in favor of parallelism. Like all discussions of specific aspects of performance, this material comes with a use-before notice. Only the actual date is missing!

6.2 Choosing Execution Mode

This book has presented the opportunity of parallelism as a major motivation for programming with streams. But until now there has been no discussion of when you should actually take that opportunity.[2] There are three sets of factors to consider.

Execution context   What is the context in which your program is executing? Remember that the implementation of parallel streams is via the common fork/join pool, which by default decides its thread count on the basis of a query to the operating system for the number of hardware cores. Operating systems vary in their responses to this query; for example, they may take account of hyperthreading, a technology that allows two threads to share a single core, so that the core does not have to idle when one thread is waiting for data. In a processor-bound application, that may very well result in parallelizing over more threads than can be used at one time.

Another aspect of the execution context is competition from other applications running on the same hardware. An implicit assumption in the common fork/join pool configuration is that there are no other demands on the hardware while parallel operations are being performed. If the machine is already heavily loaded, then either some of the fork/join pool threads will be starved of CPU time, or the performance of the other applications will be degraded.

If either of these problems means that you want to reduce the number of threads in the common fork/join pool—or indeed, if you want to change it for any other reason—the system property `java.util.concurrent.ForkJoinPool.common.parallelism` can be set to override the default configuration of the fork/join pool. Of course, if you do set this property, you then have the challenging task of justifying your change by measuring the resulting change in your application's performance!

In addition to external competition, you should consider internal competition in deciding whether to execute streams in parallel. Some applications are already highly concurrent; for example, consider a web server, which will perform best if it can assign

---

[2]Recall from §3.2.3 that all streams expose the methods `parallel` and `sequential`, which set the execution mode for an entire pipeline. That section makes the point that if there is more than one of these method calls on a single pipeline, it is the last one that decides the execution mode.

each user request to a single core for execution. That strategy is obviously incompatible with one that attempts to take over all cores for the execution of a single request.

Workload   As we saw in §5.2, a lot of machinery is required to set up parallel streams. The delay introduced by this setup needs to be balanced by the time saved subsequently by the simultaneous processing of the stream elements. Without parallelism, the elapsed execution time of a series of N tasks, each requiring Q time individually, is $N \times Q$. With perfect parallelization over P independent processors, it is $N \times Q \div P$. The difference between these two amounts must outweigh the overheads of parallelization. Clearly, the larger that N and Q are, the more likely that is to be the case. Figure 6-3 shows the relative speedup over a loop of sequential and parallel stream execution for a pure processing task of three different durations. The operation cost Q is provided by the JMH method `Blackhole.consumeCPU`. Its value varies from one machine to another; this experiment was performed on the Q8400 mentioned earlier, on which Q was measured (to give a rough idea of its value) at about five nanoseconds. Figure 6-3 shows break-even points (the crossing point of the lines) between parallel and sequential execution at values of $N \times Q$ of ~40 microseconds, around five times less than the range informally reported by the Oracle team. Figure 6-2 shows a similar $N \times Q$ response for the first stream program developed in this book, the "maxDistance" problem from §1.2.

The optimal value of P for parallel execution is not an absolute, but depends on the workload. If $N \times Q$ is insufficiently great, then the overhead of partitioning the workload will dominate the savings made by parallelization. The larger the workload, the greater will be the speedup produced by an increased processor count.[3]

Spliterator and collector performance   These are discussed in more detail in §6.7 and §6.8. For now, it is enough to notice that splitting by sources and concurrent accumulation by collectors becomes increasingly important as Q decreases; a high Q value tends to make intermediate operations into the pipeline bottleneck, making parallelism more worthwhile. In the situation where Q is low, by contrast, concurrent performance of the stream source and terminal operation become more important in deciding whether to go parallel.

One problem of applying this model lies in the difficulty of estimating Q in real-life situations, and in the fact that stream operations with high Q are unlikely to be as simple as in this experiment, as we saw in the larger examples of Chapters 4 and 5. If in fact they are, then measuring the cost of intermediate pipeline operations is straightforward and the results of this experiment will be directly useful to you; but, in practice,

---

[3] This informal statement appeals to Gustafson's law, which reframes the well-known analysis of Amdahl's law to draw a less pessimistic conclusion. In contrast to Amdahl's law, which sets very tight limits on the parallel speedup attainable with a fixed N and varying P, the scenario for Gustafson's law is one in which N scales with P, giving a constant run time (see http://www.johngustafson.net/pubs/pub13/pub13.htm).

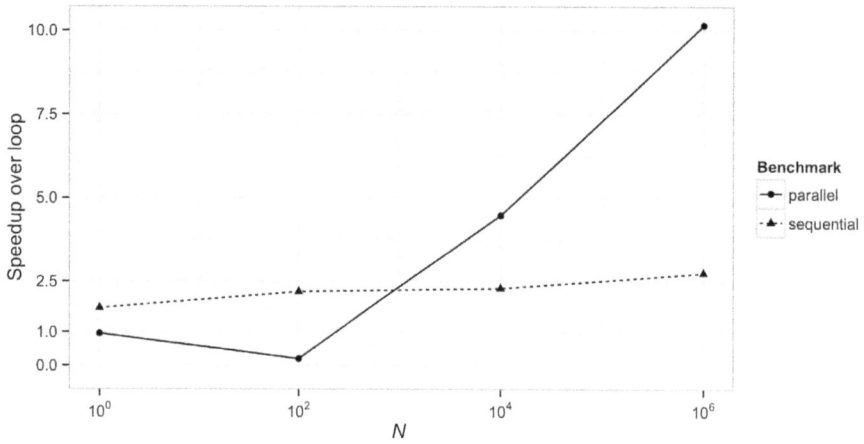

FIGURE 6-2. *"maxDistance" program performance (http://git.io/r6BtKQ)*

more complex intermediate operations will usually involve some I/O or synchronization, resulting in fewer gains from going parallel. As always, if you are in doubt, be prepared to repeat this experiment, adapting it to your own requirements.

6.3 Stream Characteristics

The preceding section represented the question of whether to go parallel very simply. This was made possible by ignoring the differences between the behavior of different streams and of different intermediate operations. In this section we will look more closely at the properties of streams, and in later sections we will see how different operations can make use of these to choose good implementation strategies—or, in some cases, be restricted by them to suboptimal strategies. For example, maintaining element ordering during parallel processing incurs a significant overhead for some intermediate and terminal operations, so if a stream's elements are known to be unordered—for example, if they are sourced from a HashSet—then stream operations can make performance gains by not preserving element ordering.

Streams expose metadata like this through *characteristics*, which can be either true or false; in this case, an operation would check whether the characteristic ORDERED was true for this stream. The characteristics of a stream *S* are initially defined by its source (in fact, stream characteristics are defined as fields of the Spliterator interface); subsequently, a new stream produced by an intermediate operation on *S* may, depending on the operation, have the same characteristics as *S*, or may have some

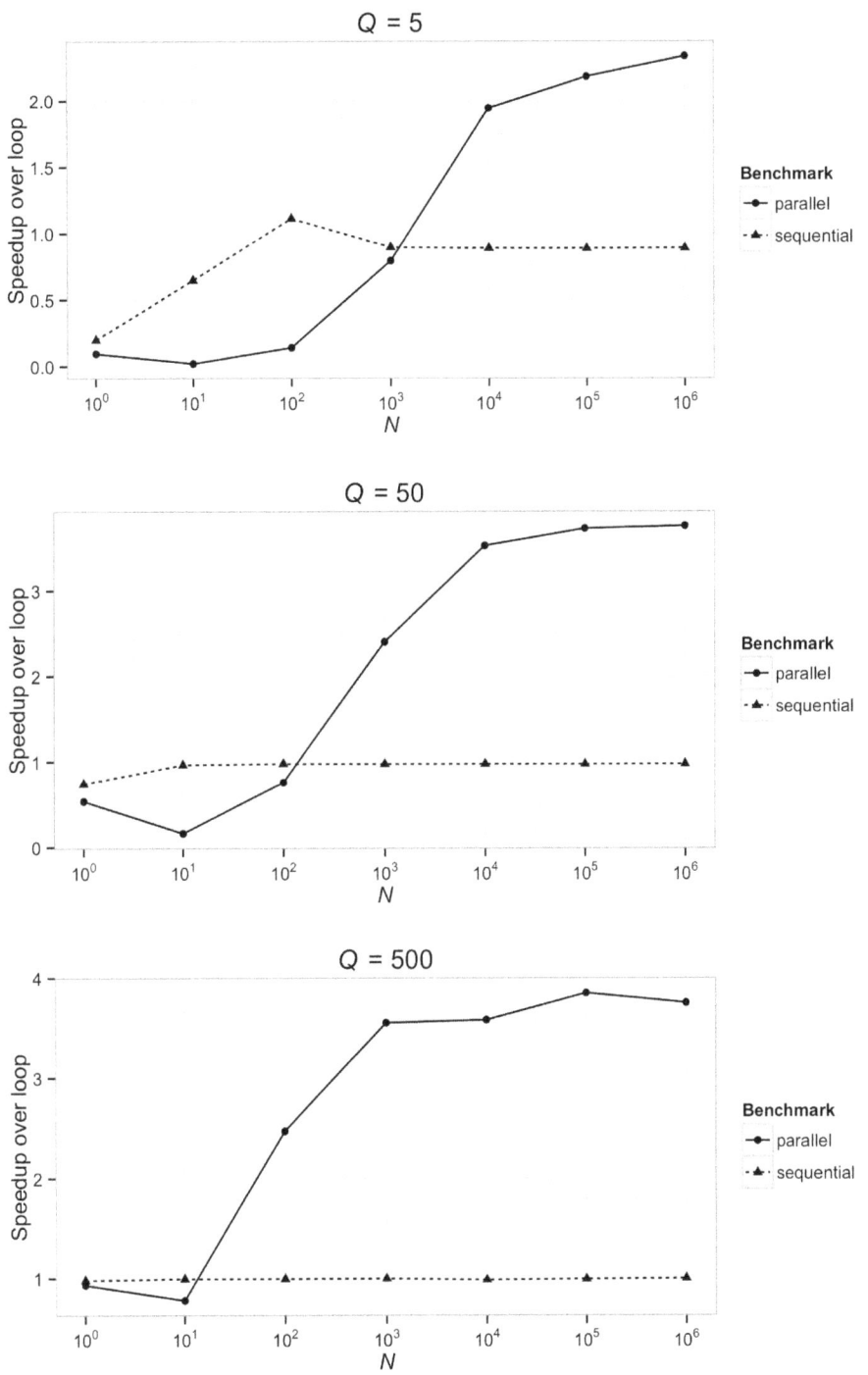

FIGURE 6-3. *Stream performance: N*Q model (http://git.io/4Nluqw)*

removed or new ones added. Here, for example, is a selection of the characteristics of each stage in a pipeline.

```
Stream.of(8, 3, 5, 6, 7, 4)          // ORDERED, SIZED
    .filter(i -> i % 2 == 0)         // ORDERED
    .sorted()                        // ORDERED, SORTED
    .distinct()                      // DISTINCT, ORDERED, SORTED
    .map(i -> i + 1)                 // ORDERED
    .unordered();                    // none
```

We will consider ORDERED in the next section; here is the meaning of the others:

- SORTED: Elements of streams with this characteristic are sorted in their natural ordering—that is, their type implements Comparable, and they have been sorted using its compareTo method. Stream elements may have been sorted in other orders if a Comparator has been defined and used for the purpose, but such streams do not have the SORTED characteristic. So, for example, a stream whose source is a NavigableSet has the characteristic SORTED, but only if the implementation was created using a default constructor rather than one that accepts a Comparator. By contrast, this characteristic will not be set in a stream sourced from a List.

  An example of the use of this characteristic is in sorting: the operation of sorting in natural order can be optimized away entirely when applied to a stream with the characteristic SORTED. For another example, distinct on a sequential sorted stream can apply a simple algorithm to avoid storing elements: an element is added to the output stream only if it is unequal to its predecessor.

- SIZED: A stream has this characteristic if the number of elements is fixed and accurately known. This is true, for example, of all streams sourced from non-concurrent collections. These must not be modified in any way during stream processing, so their size remains known. Concurrent collections, by contrast, may have elements inserted or deleted during stream processing, so the number of elements cannot be accurately predicted before the stream is exhausted. Streams from most of the non-collection stream sources in §5.1 are not sized.

  An example of an optimization that makes use of SIZED is accumulating to a collection; this is more efficient if dynamic resizing of the collection can be avoided by creating it with the appropriate size.

- DISTINCT: A stream with this characteristic will have no two elements x and y for which x.equals(y). A stream sourced from a Set will have this characteristic, but not one sourced from a List.

  For an example of its usefulness, the operation distinct can be optimized away entirely when applied to a stream with this characteristic.

6.4 Ordering

Of the characteristics listed in the previous section, ordering is the one that most deserves attention in a performance chapter, because dispensing with ordering can remove a big overhead from parallel stream processing for some pipelines. Moreover, as Chapter 1 emphasized, this is the characteristic that we are most likely to impose unnecessarily from our long familiarity with iterative processing—think of the friend in §1.1.1 who insisted that you put the letters for mailing into the letterbox in alphabetical order. So it is very much worthwhile distinguishing those cases in which ordering really does matter.

A stream is said to have an *encounter order* if the ordering of the elements is semantically significant. For example, take `List`: given a sequence of operations to add elements to a `List`, its contract specifies how those elements will be positioned and guarantees to preserve their ordering when returning them, for example by iteration. Now consider processing the elements of a `List` using a stream:

```
String joined = stringList.parallelStream()
    .map(String::toUpperCase)
    .collect(Collectors.joining());
```

You would be surprised and disappointed if the string `joined` did not reflect the ordering of `stringList`. You can think of encounter order as the property by which a stream preserves the "position" of elements passing through it. In this case because `List` has an encounter order (data structures can also have this property), so too does the stream, and the spatial arrangement of the elements is preserved into the terminal operation. For example, if `stringList` has the value `["a", "B", "c"]`, then `joined` is guaranteed to be `"ABC"`, not `"BAC"` or `"CAB"`.

By contrast, if the stream source has no encounter order—if it is a `HashSet`, say—then there is no spatial order to be preserved: the stream source has no encounter order and neither has the stream.[4] Since the stream has been explicitly identified as parallel, we must assume that the chunks of the collection may be processed by different threads on different processors. There is no guarantee that the results of processing, used by the `joining` method as soon they are available, will arrive in the order in which processing began. If your subsequent use of the concatenated string doesn't require ordering—say, for example, that you will use it only to extract the occurrence count of each character—then to specify it may hurt performance and will be confusingly at odds with the purpose of the program.

---

[4]Note that although you might expect all `Set` implementations to be intrinsically unordered, encounter order for a collection actually depends on whether the specification defines an iteration order: among the Collections Framework implementations of `Set`, that is the case for `LinkedHashSet` and for the implementations of the `Set` subinterfaces `SortedSet` and `NavigableSet`.

You should not need to understand detail of the stream class implementations to apply this general rule. For example, you might not expect that unordering a stream would improve performance in a program like this:

```
long distinctCount = stringList.parallelStream()
    .unordered()
    .distinct()
    .count();
```

but in fact performance on large data sets improves by a factor of 50 percent (http://git.io/i6frOw). The reason is that `distinct` is implemented by testing membership of the set of previously seen elements, and if the stream is unordered a concurrent map can be used. But this is an implementation detail that might well change in the future: the principle—that you should be aware of ordering and use it only when necessary—will not change.

Originally the term "encounter order" was defined in contrast to "temporal order," used to describe the situation in which the elements of a stream are ordered according to the time at which they are produced. Now that situation is described as "unordered": a shorthand way of expressing the idea not that a stream has no order, but rather that you cannot rely on the order that it has. It is easy to show that there is no necessary relationship between temporal and encounter order for parallel streams, for example by observing the effect of mutating a threadsafe object from within a pipeline operation. Executed sequentially, this code

```
AtomicInteger counter = new AtomicInteger(1);
IntStream.rangeClosed(1,5)
    .mapToObj(i -> i + ":" + counter.getAndAdd(1) + " ")
    .forEachOrdered(System.out::print);
```

usually produces the output

```
1:1 2:2 3:3 4:4 5:5
```

whereas when executed in parallel, you can never predict the ordering of side-effects:

```
AtomicInteger counter = new AtomicInteger(1);
IntStream.rangeClosed(1,5).parallel()
    .mapToObj(i -> i + ":" + counter.getAndAdd(1) + " ")
    .forEachOrdered(System.out::print);
```

produces (for example)

```
1:2 2:1 3:5 4:4 5:3
```

But notice that in neither case can you depend on the order of side-effects.

6.5 Stateful and Stateless Operations

Intuitively, it is clear that some intermediate operations lend themselves more easily to parallelization than others. For example, the application of `map` to a stream can obviously be implemented by an element-by-element evaluation of `map`'s behavioral parameter applied to the stream elements. By contrast, `sorted`, the operation of sorting the elements of a stream, cannot complete until it has accumulated all the values that the stream will yield before exhaustion. Because `map` can process each stream element without reference to any other, it is said to be *stateless*. Other stateless stream operations include `filter`, `flatMap`, and the variants of `map` and `flatMap` that produce primitive streams. Pipelines containing exclusively stateless operations can be processed in a single pass, whether sequential or parallel, with little or no data buffering.

Operations like `sorted`, which do need to retain information about already-processed values, are called *stateful*. Stateful operations store some, or even—if multiple passes are required—all, of the stream data in memory. Other stateful operations include `distinct` and the stream truncation operations `skip` and `limit`. The library implementations use various strategies to avoid in-memory buffering where possible; these make it very difficult to predict how a stateful operation will influence parallel speedup. For example, a naïve benchmark measuring the performance of `sorted` on a stream of `Integer` can report parallel speedup of 2.5 on four cores (http://git.io/6kdkDw) where the conditions happen to be right for optimization. On the other hand, the Oracle team experienced frustration with the unexpected and unintuitive difficulty of efficiently parallelizing `limit`, which remains an operation to use with caution in a parallel stream. Fortunately, further work on the stream library, implementing further optimizations and changing existing ones, will continually improve the situation for library users.

6.6 Boxing and Unboxing

An important motivation for the introduction of primitive streams was to avoid boxing and unboxing overheads. In §3.1.2, we considered a simple task to manipulate number streams. One program used a primitive stream:

```
OptionalInt max = IntStream.rangeClosed(1,5)
    .map(i -> i + 1)
    .max();
```

and the other a stream of wrapper values:

```
Optional<Integer> max = Arrays.asList(1,2,3,4,5).stream()
    .map(i -> i + 1)
    .max(Integer::compareTo);
```

The performance of these two programs is compared for different stream lengths in Figure 6-4, which includes, for reference, a similar comparison for iterative programs. As expected, the code without boxing easily outperforms the boxed code; for large data sets the speedup approaches an order of magnitude.

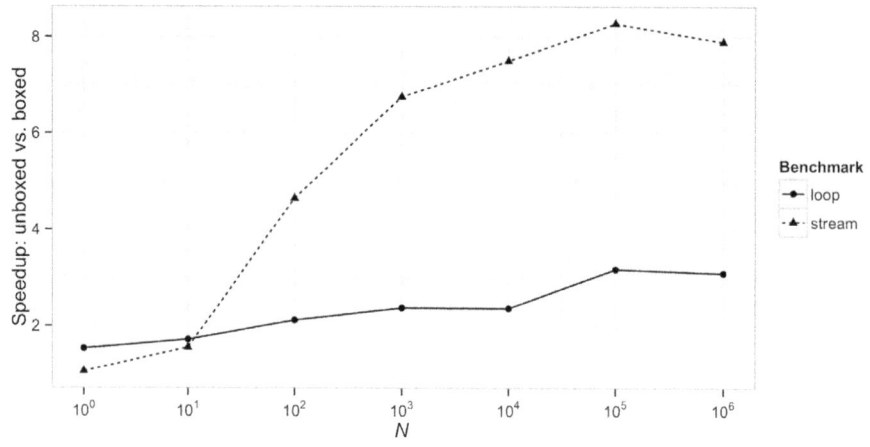

FIGURE 6-4. *Unboxed vs. boxed performance (http://git.io/YB9V6g)*

6.7 Spliterator Performance

The influence of the stream source on sequential stream performance is relatively straightforward: if the source can provide values quickly enough to keep the stream processes supplied with data, it will have little influence on performance. If not, it will form the bottleneck on the overall process. For parallel streams, the question is more complex, since two complementary processes—splitting and iteration—are needed to decompose the source data to supply parallel threads. A data source may provide a fast implementation of one but be unable to support the other efficiently. For example, `IntStream.iterate` may be able to deliver values extremely quickly if its `UnaryOperator` is efficient, but since each value cannot be calculated until its predecessor is known, it provides little opportunity for splitting, so parallel streams using it as a source may show no speedup over sequential execution. Among common stream sources, the most efficiently splittable are arrays, `ArrayList`, `HashMap`, and `ConcurrentHashMap`. The worst are `LinkedList`, `BlockingQueue` implementations, and I/O-based sources.

Stream-bearing I/O methods and others like `iterate` can sometimes benefit from parallelization, however, if an extra processing step is inserted, pre-buffering their output in an in-memory data structure, as the discussion of `BufferedReader` (p. 115) suggested. Generalizing, this leads to the conclusion that programs using the Stream API will gain most from parallel speedup when their data source is an in-memory, random-access structure lending itself to efficient splitting. (Of course, that does not prevent programs with other data sources benefiting from the Stream API in other ways.)

A realistically sized example that illustrates this is the program of Chapter 5 simulating `grep -b`. Reading a sequentially accessed file into a `MappedByteBuffer` brings the data into a highly suitable form for parallelization. An experiment to measure the performance of this program (http://git.io/-CziKQ) compares the speed of splitting a `MappedByteBuffer` into lines by three different algorithms: iterative, stream sequential, and stream parallel. The overhead of setting up the `MappedByteBuffer` is excluded from the measurements in order to focus on the efficiency of the splitting algorithm. The results are relatively independent of the data set size: sequential stream processing is between 1.9 and 2.0 times as fast as iterative processing for files of between 10,000 and a million lines; over the same range, parallel processing is between 5.2 and 5.4 times as fast as iterative processing. This is unsurprising, given the efficient splitting algorithm developed in §5.4.

6.8 Collector Performance

The behavior of terminal operations, like that of stream sources, is more complex for parallel than for sequential streams. In the sequential case, collection consists only of calling the collector's accumulator function, which, if it consumes values from the stream quickly enough, can avoid being a bottleneck for the entire process. For parallel streams, the framework treats collectors differently according to whether they declare themselves CONCURRENT, by means of the characteristics by which collectors report their properties. A concurrent collector guarantees that its accumulator operation is threadsafe, so that the framework does not need to take responsibility for avoiding concurrent accumulator calls as it must do for non-threadsafe structures. In principle, avoiding the framework overhead of managing thread confinement should lead to better parallel performance. This can be realized in practice, as we shall see, by choosing appropriate data sets and configuration parameters.

Collectors report only two other characteristics besides CONCURRENT: a collector can have IDENTITY_FINISH, which tells the framework that it need not make provision for a finisher function, and UNORDERED, which tells the framework that there is no need to maintain an encounter order on the stream, as the collector will discard it anyway.

6.8.1 Concurrent Map Merge

The concurrent collectors provided by the library are obtained from the various overloads of the `Collector` methods `toConcurrentMap` and `groupingByConcurrent`. Those that use a framework-supplied `ConcurrentMap` implementation (rather than allowing you to provide a `ConcurrentMap` supplier) all rely on `ConcurrentHashMap` (CHM). The performance characteristics of these collectors need some explanation, which all potential users of these collectors should understand. A naïve benchmark (http://git.io/YXyvpg) shows worse performance for `groupingByConcurrent` than for `groupingBy` for any data set. Profiling shows that `groupingByConcurrent` is slowed by frequent resizing of the CHM; creating the CHM with an initial size sufficient to avoid resizing improves performance by about 30 percent, even for a data set of only 1000 elements. If the comparison is made fair, however—that is, if the initial size of the `HashMap` used by `groupingBy` is also increased—it is still unfavorable to `groupingByConcurrent`, since resizing is a major overhead for `HashMap` as well.

But we are now in more familiar territory, in which a slower process—in this case, adding an element to CHM as against adding one to `HashMap`—is compensated for large data sets by the ability to perform the slower operation in parallel. With presizing chosen to achieve a load factor of 0.5 (http://git.io/HAiaQQ), the relative performance shows a pattern, by now familiar, of parallel speedup increasing with increased data size past 100,000 elements (Figure 6-5).

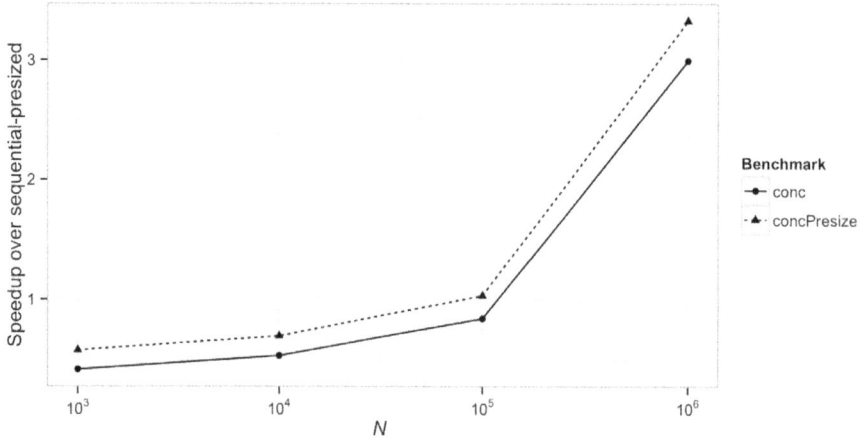

FIGURE 6-5. *groupingByConcurrent* vs. *groupingBy*

In fact, Figure 6-5 still does not tell the whole story. Sequential `groupingBy` creates new objects, so garbage collection becomes a factor in performance. Parallel GC biases the experiment in favor of sequential `groupingBy` because the cores unused by the sequential operation are available to run GC in parallel, hiding its cost. Running the same test with four measurement threads (supplying the option `-t 4` to JMH) results in a break-even point below 10,000 elements.

6.8.2 Performance Analysis: Point Grouping

The "point grouping" collector of §4.3 is designed to be a good case for parallelization; although the data structure being created is a linked series of non-threadsafe `ArrayDeques`, all the collector operations on them are fast, with no iteration involved, so there is relatively little contention during the collection process. Run sequentially, the program of §4.3 (http://git.io/XdvZ3w) has a very similar performance profile to its iterative equivalent; the speedup of parallel over sequential execution is about 1.8 for a stream with no payload on a four-core machine, rising to 2.5 for a payload of 100 JMH tokens per element.

6.8.3 Performance Analysis: Finding My Books

The last collector program to be analyzed here is from §4.3.2: it is the program to find the displacement of each of my books along its shelf, given the page count of the preceding volumes. Following the analysis of concurrent map merging (§6.8.1), we should not be surprised to find that this collector, which is specified to produce a map, must be used with caution as the terminal operation for a parallel stream. Indeed, as it stands, the program (http://git.io/aMoy6w) is slower than the equivalent iterative version by about 40 percent. Several elements contribute to this, each of which might be mitigated in a real-life situation:

- This problem is an example of a *prefix sum*, in which the value of every element depends on the values of the preceding ones. In a naïve parallel algorithm for prefix sum, like this one, the total cost of the combine operations (that is, the total delay imposed by them) is proportional to the size of the input data set, regardless of the level of parallelism in use.[5] The gravity of this problem depends on the cost of the combine operation; in this case, streaming the right-hand `Deque` into an intermediate `List` imposes an overhead that reduces speedup, for an intermediate workload, by about 20 percent compared to a simple iterative updating of the right-hand `Deque` before it is merged with the left-hand one.

- The finisher accumulates the results into a `ConcurrentHashMap`, whose initial size is currently left at the default value (16). For a realistically sized data set,

---

[5]Java 8 provided `java.util.Arrays` with various overloads of a new method `parallelPrefix` for computing prefix sums efficiently, but this innovation has not yet reached the Stream API.

this will result in numerous resizes, expensive for `ConcurrentHashMap` and one that generates a great deal of garbage—in fact, garbage collection costs dominate the unrefined program, so performance measurements do not give a useful indication of its performance in isolation. Presizing the CHM provides the biggest single contribution to improving performance. Even so, collecting to a `Map` is always an expensive operation; if the problem specified a linear data structure to hold the result, allowing the finisher simply to be omitted, parallel speedup over iterative processing would increase by about 40 percent for the same workload.

- The program as presented in Chapter 4 does no processing on the `Book` objects before they are collected. In this, it places parallel stream processing at a possibly unrealistic disadvantage—in real-life situations, preprocessing before collection will usually be required. As with all parallel stream programs, the greater the proportion of program workload that can be executed by intermediate operations using the fork/join pool, the greater the parallel speedup that can be achieved.

When these three changes are applied (http://git.io/wZe_tg), the parallel stream program shows a speedup of 2.5 (for four cores) over the sequential version, for a data set of a million elements, each requiring 200 JMH tokens to process.

6.9 Conclusion

The last example emphasizes again that the parallelization mechanism of the Stream API is by no means bound to produce performance improvement. To achieve that, your application must fall into the focus area for fork/join—CPU-bound processing of in-memory, random-access data—and must satisfy the other conditions discussed in this chapter, including the requirements for sufficiently high data set size and per-element processing cost. Fork/join parallelism is no silver bullet; the good news, however, is that your investment in writing parallel-ready code will not be wasted, whatever the outcome of your performance analysis. Your code will be better and, when advances in technology change the cost-benefit balance of going parallel, it will—as the name suggests—be ready.

CHAPTER

7

API Evolution with Default Methods

D efault methods allow interfaces to define behavior. Why did we need this change, and what are its consequences? The short answer to the first question is: to support API evolution. The need for this has been felt for a long time, but became pressing with the requirement for stream support in collections. (The longer answer is that, once introduced, default methods have other uses as well, as we shall see.) The Java Collections Framework—like its extensions, for example Google Guava—is strongly interface-based: that is, the capabilities of a collection are (with some exceptions) defined by the Javadoc contract of its interface. For the existing collections library to be enhanced to support streams, interface methods like `Collection.stream` were needed. The alternative—complete replacement of the Java Collections Framework—would have presented extremely unattractive problems of compatibility and code maintenance.

So it was decided to change the situation in which adding methods to existing interfaces created unmanageable compatibility problems. Reviewing these problems will help us understand the choices that the designers made in implementing that decision. Consider, for example, adding an abstract method `stream` to `Collection`. (But note that the problem described here applies to all published interfaces, not just those in the platform library.) Prior to Java 8, `Collection` declared only abstract methods:

```
public interface Collection<E> {
    int size();
    boolean isEmpty();
    // 11 more abstract method declarations
}
```

and a class implemented the interface only if it overrode every abstract method declaration with a concrete method:

```
class CustomCollection<E> implements Collection<E> {
    public int size() { ... }
    public boolean isEmpty() { ... }
    // 11 more concrete method declarations
}
```

Now consider the problem of making collections into stream sources. The interface `Collection` had to be extended with a method `stream`; without default methods, that could be done only by adding an abstract method declaration:

```
public interface Collection<E> {
    int size();
    boolean isEmpty();
    // 11 more abstract methods
    Stream<E> stream();       // abstract method - not added in reality
}
```

If the implementation CustomCollection were now compiled against this new version of Collection, the result would be a *source incompatibility*: compilation would fail because Collection now declares an abstract method not overridden by CustomCollection. Without default methods, the only fix would be to make CustomCollection match the new definition of Collection by adding a concrete overriding declaration of stream. But if the interface is part of a library—Collection is particularly widely used, but any published API could be an example—then it would be hardly practicable to accompany its every enhancement with a requirement for extensive source changes to all its implementations.

Note that, without recompilation, existing bytecode for CustomCollection could still link to and run against the new version of Collection—interface and implementation would be *binary compatible*, according to the Java Language Specification (§13.2). But leaving the implementation unchanged would only transfer the problem to the client programmer: now, client code written to take advantage of the advertised new capability of the interface would compile without problems:

```
Collection<Integer> c = new CustomCollection<>();
Stream<Integer> s = c.stream();
```

but would fail at run time with an AbstractMethodError.

The basic problem was that the traditional role of a Java interface was restricted to helping define a contract between client and implementation; the responsibility for providing the functionality promised by the contract lay entirely with the implementation. Naturally, if the requirements of a supply contract are extended, the supplier must be aware of the change and must fulfill the new part. Once an interface has been published, however, it becomes impracticable to insist on this for all implementations. As a result, published interfaces are never extended with abstract methods.

The introduction of default methods changed this situation by extending the role of the interface beyond the definition of a contract to include its partial implementation. Interfaces can now include code, in the bodies of two kinds of non-abstract methods: *default methods* and *static methods*. Default methods are now central to API evolution; for example, this is how Collection.stream is actually declared in Java 8:

```
public interface Collection<E> {
    int size();
    boolean isEmpty();
    // 11 more abstract methods
    default Stream<E> stream() {
        // delegate to spliterator, also a default method of Collection
        return StreamSupport.stream(spliterator(), false);
    }
    // other default methods
}
```

For a client, the interface still has the same meaning: it defines a type and lists the declarations of the methods that a client can call on that type. For an implementation, the main element of its relationship with the interface is also unchanged: it is still required to override the abstract method declarations with concrete ones. A new element is added to the interface-implementation relationship, however: the implementation can now choose to override default method declarations—because these are virtual—and replace or modify their behaviors, just as in traditional Java instance method overriding.

So now an interface can be extended to allow client code to call new methods without requiring any immediate change in existing implementations. This removes a serious block on API evolution, present ever since JDK1.0. It is worth asking why this block was allowed to remain in place for so long.

Aside from the considerable practical difficulties in making a change of this size, attitudes to multiple inheritance had to change. Aversion to multiple inheritance was a strong element in the original design of Java because of the difficulties that it had brought to other languages, most prominently to C++ in the form of the "diamond problem" (p. 169). Even so, multiple inheritance of interfaces has always been considered acceptable because interfaces were essentially type definitions, and multiple inheritance of *types* did not involve the same problems. Introducing default methods extends the role of interfaces to provide *behavior*, so multiple inheritance of behavior would now have to be allowed. The Java 8 designers were able to devise rules that make the problems with behavior inheritance manageable; the classic problems of multiple inheritance are associated with inheritance of *state*, which Java does not and never will support.

7.1 Using Default Methods

After a change as big as this, it takes time for the best new idioms to emerge. Some use cases can be seen in the Java 8 platform classes already, however. Here are four of them:

- **Methods intended to be overridden** The previous section presented methods like `Collection.stream` as the central use case for default methods. The implementation of `stream` is delegated to another default method, `spliterator` (defined in `Iterable`, the superinterface of `Collection`). The purpose of this method is to return a spliterator that takes advantage of the structure of the collection to partition its contents for processing by different threads, like the `MappedByteBuffer` spliterator of §5.4. Of course, the default implementation itself cannot fulfill that intention; it is suboptimal for most `Collection` classes because it has no knowledge of the structure of the object it is splitting. Virtual method dispatch allows `Collection` implementations to override spliterator with concrete method definitions that take advantage of their specific features.

- **Methods that will commonly not be overridden** Some interfaces contain method declarations that will be commonly implemented by the same concrete method. For example, the default implementation of Comparator returned by Comparator.thenComparing(Comparator) is implemented very simply: first evaluating the receiver of thenComparing on its arguments, and, if it returns zero, then—as the name implies—evaluating the supplied Comparator. It is hard to see how a particular implementation could improve on this.

  A contrasting example is Iterator.remove. It's debatable whether the interface should have originally included this method, unsupported as it is by so many implementations. Nevertheless, the problem was at least mitigated in Java 8 by making remove into a default method:

```
public interface Iterator<E> {
    default void remove() {
        throw new UnsupportedOperationException("remove");
    }
    ...
}
```

  taking away the requirement to reproduce concrete boilerplate code in every Iterator implementation not supporting remove.

- **Auxiliary methods** Although a functional interface has exactly one abstract method to define its central purpose, there is no restriction on how many default methods it may have. These can be useful for adding extra capabilities. For example, we have seen Predicate and its specialized variants used to define truth-valued functions for filtering streams. You will often want to operate on the results of these truth-valued functions using the standard boolean operators AND, OR, and NOT. So Predicate and its variants declare default methods implementing these operators:

```
Predicate tolkien = b -> b.getAuthors().contains("Tolkien");
Predicate lotr = b -> b.getTitle().contains("Lord");
Predicate old = b -> b.getPubDate().isBefore(Year.of(1960));
boolean firstLotrEdn = library.stream()
    .filter(tolkien.and(lotr).and(old))
    .findAny().isPresent();
```

- **Convenience methods**: Default methods provide opportunities to relocate existing functionality in more appropriate places. For example, to sort a List in reverse natural order before Java 8, you had to call two static `Collections` methods:

```
Collections.sort(integerList,Collections.reverseOrder());
```

Now, however, the default method `List.sort` (together with a static interface method `Comparator.reverseOrder`) allows this code to be rewritten in a more readable way:

```
integerList.sort(Comparator.reverseOrder());
```

In fact, `List.sort` is more than a convenience; it allows the `List` class to override `sort` with an efficient implementation, using knowledge of its internal representation that is unavailable to the static method `Collections.sort`.

These are examples of interface methods making existing functionality much more discoverable: a `sort` method for `List` instances and a factory method for creating `Comparators` are clearly much better placed in these interfaces than in the general-purpose collections utility class `Collections`.

7.2 What Role for Abstract Classes?

Adding implementation capability to interfaces brings their role nearer to that of abstract classes, which also mix abstract method declarations with implementation capability. It is natural to ask what role remains for abstract classes.

It is easiest to understand the answer to that question in relation to a conventional Java API, containing interface, abstract class, and concrete implementations. For example, suppose that the library system of earlier chapters is to be made more general, by adding ebooks and audiobooks: these have titles and authors, but lack some properties of physical books—for example, height and page count. A refactored domain design might look in part like this:

```
interface BookIntf  {
    String getTitle();
    List<String> getAuthors();
    // other abstract methods
}
abstract class AbstractBook implements BookIntf  {
    private String title;
    private List<String> authors;
    // other fields common to physical and ebooks
    // together with getters and setters for these fields
}
class PaperBook extends AbstractBook {
```

```
    private int[] pageCounts;
    public int[] getPageCounts() { return pageCounts; }
    // other fields and getter/setter methods for physical books
}
```

Now suppose that we want to expose a method on `BookIntf` that will return the names of its authors concatenated into a single string. That would fall into the category of convenience methods described in the previous section:

```
interface BookIntf {
    default String getAuthorsAsString() {
        return getAuthors().stream().collect(joining(","));
    }
    ...
}
```

This works as a default method because it can be defined entirely in terms of another interface method, `getAuthors`. By contrast, to define `getAuthors` itself requires access to instance data, which cannot be declared in the interface. The data that is common to different subclasses, like `authors` in this example, is still held in the abstract class, which is therefore also the location for getters and setters:

```
abstract class AbstractBook implements BookIntf  {
    private List<String> authors;
    public String getAuthors() {
        return authors;
    }
    ...
}
```

The need for instance state, as in this example, is the main reason for continuing to use abstract classes. There are other limitations to default methods that mean that abstract classes are still needed: default methods can only be implemented in terms of methods on the same interface (together with accessible static methods on any type). Further, abstract methods can declare protected state and methods to share with their subclasses; this option is not available to interfaces, all of whose declarations are automatically public.

7.3 Default Method Syntax

We have already seen the form of default method declarations. They are very similar to concrete method declarations in classes. In interfaces, they are distinguished from abstract method declarations by the presence of the modifier `default` and by the fact that their body is represented by a block rather than a semicolon. Lively debate took place over whether the `default` keyword should be mandatory, given that it is not needed to make the syntax unambiguous—an interface method declaration with a block body can only be a default method. One advantage of making it mandatory is that it immediately prompts a reader's understanding, in the same way as the modifier `abstract` (also not strictly necessary) does for abstract methods and classes.

The main syntactic difference between default methods and concrete instance methods is in the modifiers that they are allowed—or, in the case of `default`, required—to have. Obviously, default methods may not be declared `abstract` or `static`, since these keywords distinguish the other kinds of interface methods (we will explore static interface methods in §7.5). They may not be declared `final`, because they must always be overridable by instance methods, as we shall see in the next section. Like all interface methods, they may be declared `public` but are implicitly public anyway; no other accessibility is possible.

The keyword `this` has its usual meaning; it refers to the current object, referenced using the type of the interface. For example, the method `Iterator.forEachRemaining` has the following implementation (slightly simplified for presentation):

```
default void forEach(Consumer<T> action) {
    for (T t : this) {
        action.accept(t);
    }
}
```

The keyword `super` is also allowed, but only when it is qualified by the name of a superinterface, as the next section explains.

Interfaces are not allowed to declare a default method with the same signature as any of the methods of `Object`. So, for example, you cannot redefine `Object.toString` in an interface. This is in line with the principles for default method inheritance that we will explore in the next section: the most important of these principles dictates that default methods can never override instance methods, whether inherited or not.

7.4 Default Methods and Inheritance

We have seen the uses and benefits of default methods; what are the drawbacks? The challenge facing the language designers in introducing them was to devise a system for method inheritance that would be simple and unambiguous while minimizing compatibility issues (and unwanted interaction with other features). The most important compatibility problem to solve concerned resolution of method calls when a choice of implementations is available, especially when these include both a concrete method inherited from a superclass and one or more default methods inherited from interfaces. The language specification rules for method call resolution are complex, but they are carefully designed so that they can be understood by reference to two simple principles.

The first principle ensures that *instance methods are chosen in preference to default methods*. This is sometimes stated as "classes win over interfaces." For example, in the following code `FooBar` inherits the method `hello` from both the interface `Foo` and the superclass `Bar`:

```
// competing instance and default method declarations of hello()

interface Foo { default String hello() { return "Foo"; } }
class Bar { public String hello() { return "Bar"; } }

class FooBar extends Bar implements Foo {
    public static void main(String[] args) {
        System.out.print("Hello from " + new FooBar().hello());
    }
}
```

When `FooBar.main` is run, the output is `Hello from Bar`. This principle holds whether the instance method is declared within the class or inherited from a super-class, and whether the instance method is abstract or concrete. The motivation for this rule is to prevent *behavioral incompatibility*: that is, the addition of a default method resulting in a change in the behavior of an implementing class. If classes always win, then a class calling a method inherited from a superclass will continue to call that method even when one of the interfaces it implements introduces a matching method declaration of its own.

The second principle ensures that if more than one competing default method is inherited by a class, the non-overridden default method* is selected. By "non-overridden method" (this is not a standard term) we mean a default method not overridden by any other that is also inherited by the class. For example:

```
// competing default method declarations of hello():
// Bar.hello() overrides Foo.hello(), so is a non-overridden method

interface Foo { default String hello() { return "Foo"; } }
interface Bar extends Foo { default String hello() { return "Bar"; } }

class FooBar implements Foo, Bar {
    public static void main(String[] args) {
        System.out.print("Hello from " + new FooBar().hello());
    }
}
```

Again, when `FooBar.main` is run, the output is `Hello from Bar`.

Of course, there may be no single non-overridden default method, if more than one default method inherited by the class is not overridden by any other. For example:

```
// competing default method declarations of hello():
// neither overrides the other

interface Foo { default String hello() { return "Foo"; } }
interface Bar { default String hello() { return "Bar"; } }

class FooBar implements Foo, Bar {
    public static void main(String[] args) {
        System.out.print(new FooBar().hello());
    }
}
```

In this case, `FooBar` fails to compile, with the error message

```
Error: class FooBar inherits unrelated defaults for hello() from      ↵
                                          types Foo and Bar
```

That is a reasonable response; the compiler has no basis for choosing between the two inherited methods, so prompts you to disambiguate the call. You can do this by making `FooBar` itself override `hello`, using a syntactic form (already present in Java, but until now only used for a different purpose in inner classes) provided to allow selection of one of the competing methods:

```
class FooBar implements Foo, Bar {
    public String hello() {
        return Bar.super.hello();
    }
}
```

The same syntax can also be used in the body of an interface default method. Note that it can only be used to resolve a conflict, not to override either of the two main principles. So you cannot use it to select a method that is not non-overridden:

```
// Foo.hello() is overridden by Bar.hello(), which is inherited by FooBar

interface Foo { default String hello() { return "Foo"; } }
interface Bar extends Foo { default String hello() { return "Bar"; } }

class FooBar implements Bar {
    public String hello() {
        return Foo.super.hello(); // illegal
    }
}
```

```
}
```

Even if `FooBar` implements both `Foo` and `Bar` directly, `Foo.hello` is not a non-overridden method and cannot be selected using the `super` syntax.

How do these principles help to resolve the "diamond problem"? This is the situation in which a class inherits a declaration by two different routes:

```
interface Apex { default String hello() { return "Apex"; } }
interface Foo extends Apex {}
interface Bar extends Apex {}

class FooBar implements Foo, Bar {
    public static void main(String[] args) {
        System.out.print(new FooBar().hello());
    }
}
```

The problem gets its name from the shape of the class diagram:

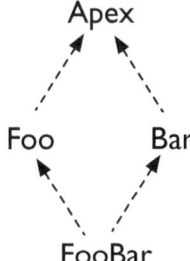

The principles of this section provide a straightforward interpretation of this scenario and its variants: in the code shown, the implementation of `hello` inherited by `FooBar` is the one defined by `Apex`; there is no other possibility. If, however, `Foo` or `Bar` is now changed to also declare a default implementation of `hello`, that method becomes the one inherited by `FooBar`, on the "non-overridden method" principle. Notice that the this principle, combined with virtual method dispatch, can give apparently surprising results in this situation. For example, if in the preceding code the declaration of `Foo` was changed to

```
interface Foo extends Apex { default String hello() { return "Foo"; } }
```

then this code

```
Bar bar = new FooBar();
System.out.println("Hello from " + bar.hello());
```

would produce the output `Hello from Foo`. The static type of `bar` is unimportant; what counts is that it refers to an instance of `FooBar`, whose non-overridden method is inherited from `Foo`.

If both `Foo` and `Bar` declare default implementations, then they conflict, and `FooBar` must provide an overriding declaration.

7.4.1 Compatibility Problems

The principles of the preceding section cover the great majority of practical situations. Unfortunately, it is not always possible to avoid incompatibilities. This section describes three problematic situations.

In the following code, `Intf` represents a published interface, and `Impl` a library implementation. They are not necessarily in the same library, so the maintainers of `Intf` may well know nothing about its implementations, and cannot take their declarations into account in evolving the API.

```
interface Intf {
    // various abstract and default methods
}
class Impl implements Intf {
    // implementation of various abstract methods in Intf
    public String hello(long l) { return "Foo"; }
}
class Client {
    public static void main(String[] args) {
        System.out.println("Hello from " + new Impl().hello(3));
    }
}
```

In this version, running `Client.main` obviously results in the output `Hello from Impl`. We now consider two different changes to `Intf`, each of which adds a method to `Intf` that *almost* matches the declaration of `Impl.hello`. For example, `Intf` could declare a version of `hello` with the same signature but an incompatible return type:

```
interface Intf {
    default void hello(long l) { }
    ...
}
```

Between overriding methods, classes always win; but this is not an overriding method. Compiling `Impl` against the new version of `Intf` produces this message:

```
Error: foo(long) in Impl cannot implement foo(long) in Intf
return type java.lang.String is not compatible with void
```

A variation of this problem occurs if `Impl`'s declaration of `hello` is non-public; in this case, even if the signature of the new method in `Intf` matches exactly, it will—since interface methods are automatically public—cause the compiler to report that `Impl`'s override is attempting to narrow access to `hello`.

The second problem is more serious. Here, the interface adds a default method declaration with a parameter whose type is assignment compatible with a corresponding parameter in the existing declaration. In this example, the new declaration might be:

```
interface Intf {
    default String hello(int l) { return "Intf"; }
    ...
}
```

According to the rules for method overloading, this declares a new overload of `hello`, which, since it does not override the existing one, is inherited by `Impl`. So both the new and the old method overloads are available for the call of `hello(3)` from `Client` and, when `Client` is compiled, the *most specific* one is chosen, as defined by the Java Language Specification (§15.12). Since 3 is an int, not a long, the newly inherited overload is more specific, and the output will now be `Hello from Intf`. The change in behavior takes place without any change in `Impl`! This example illustrates the difficulty of making fully compatible language changes in the face of already complex semantic rules. (Method overloading is notoriously difficult in this respect, as we also saw in §2.8.)

A different kind of behavioral incompatibility is unrelated to syntax problems but is inherent to dynamic method dispatch. A newly-introduced supertype method may be unable to respect the invariants of an implementing class, because it has no knowledge of them. For a real-life case, consider `Map.putIfAbsent`, introduced in Java 8:

```
default V putIfAbsent(K key, V value) {
    V v = get(key);
    if (v == null) {
        v = put(key, value);
    }
    return v;
}
```

This method, if not overridden, will destroy the thread safety of any implementing `Map`: between the time at which a thread evaluates the test and the time at which it executes the action, the value of `v` could have been set by another thread. The current thread would then overwrite that value, contrary to the specification of the method. There is no true solution to this problem; in the worst case, as here, all implementations must be inspected to ensure that they override newly introduced default methods.

Notice that the problems of this section aren't new: any of them could occur with class inheritance. What makes them more serious is that, whereas it is expected and understood that changes in a class hierarchy are liable to cause problems like these, it is new for Java that interface changes can have these effects. Fortunately, they do not often occur in practice.

7.5 Static Methods in Interfaces

Once the decision had been made to allow interfaces to provide behavior, it was natural to examine static methods to see if they also could, or should, be allowed into interfaces. With hindsight, it's easy to see the advantages of permitting them: throughout this book we have been taking advantage of their presence with method calls like

```
Stream.of(1,2,3);
Comparator.naturalOrder();
```

With the perspective of the preceding section of this chapter, however, we can see the importance of minimizing compatibility problems. Actually, these can be eliminated altogether for static interface methods by restricting the syntax that can be used for referencing them to the specific form *DeclaringInterface.MethodName*. (Obviously, this solution wasn't available for default methods, since it's not compatible with virtual method dispatch.) So one difference from static class methods is that static interface methods are not inherited:

```
interface Bar {static void barHello() {} }
class Foo { static void fooHello() {} }

class FooBar extends Foo implements Bar {
    public static void main(String[] args) {
        fooHello();            // invoke inherited method
        barHello();            // illegal - doesn't compile
        Bar.barHello();        // only legal way to reference barHello
    }
}
```

For the same reason, you cannot refer to static interface methods by the syntax *ObjectReference.MethodName*.[1] In other respects, static interface methods are declared in the same way, and have essentially the same properties as static class methods. Like other interface methods, they may be declared `public` but are implicitly

---

[1] The two differences with static class methods—preventing inheritance, and disallowing calls through object references—are probably best seen as a refusal to repeat two mistakes.

public anyway. It is not permitted to declare a static interface method `final`, since that would be a meaningless modifier for a method that cannot be inherited anyway.

7.5.1 Using Static Methods

Again, it is too soon to know what idioms in API design will emerge to make use of static interface methods. In Java 8, the platform classes expose them as factory methods—as with `Stream.of`, `Collector.of`, and `Comparator.comparing`—and as ways of locating functionality that are often an improvement on the traditional use of utility classes.

Utility classes can present major difficulties in locating functionality. The most extreme example in the platform library, `java.util.Collections`, contains more than 60 static methods, of which the majority are associated not with collections in general but with one of `Set`, `List`, `Queue`, or `Map` (the last of which is not even a sub-type of `Collection`). A newcomer to the Java Collections Framework cannot deduce in any systematic way where to find a factory method for producing, say, a `Map` in-stance. Such arbitrary allocation of function is a major obstacle to learning an API. By contrast, now that interfaces can expose methods like `Comparator.comparing` and `Stream.of`, they can be where a developer would naturally expect to find them. This improvement is not restricted to new methods; for example, Java 8 introduces a factory method `Comparator.reverseOrder`, which is implemented simply by delegation to the existing (but poorly located) method `Collections.reverseOrder`.

That said, it is unlikely that utility classes like `Collections` will altogether dis-appear in new APIs. Consider the interface `Collector`; there are more than 40 fac-tory methods for this interface in the Stream API. Only two have been declared as static methods of the interface itself, namely the two general-purpose overloads of `Collector.of` that were discussed in §4.3. The forty-odd other predefined factory methods, described in §4.1, deserve and get a class—`Collectors`—of their own; putting them all into the `Collector` interface would overwhelm its core function. This example leads us to expect that a balance of usage between static interface methods and utility classes will emerge over time.

7.6 Conclusion

It is no easy task to change a programming language that has been in widespread use for nearly for two decades. When the feature to be changed is as central to the language as interfaces are to Java, then the problem is even more difficult. Despite the problems described in this chapter, the addition of behavior to Java interfaces has, overall, caused remarkably few difficulties.

This is partly because the features have been strictly tailored to the purpose of enabling API evolution. Some of the controversy around the introduction of default methods was based on expectations that they would reproduce features like traits or mixins in other languages. The absence of state in interfaces prevents that, however. Similarly, as we have seen in this chapter, expectations that interfaces could now replace abstract classes, or make utility classes redundant, are exaggerated. But they do fulfil the purpose of their design, to enable API evolution; the opportunities that this opens up, initially benefiting the Stream API, will create possibilities for maintaining and enhancing other APIs far beyond what has been feasible until now.

Conclusion

I should like to end this book on a personal note. I have long since lost count of the technologies that I have seen, over four decades, announced as the future of the industry, only to be forgotten within a year or two. A much smaller number have been slow burners: technologies that have grown a faithful following without ever reaching the commercial mainstream. In this category, one that stands out is functional programming, which has attracted some of the best minds and produced some of the best ideas in software development while remaining a minority interest.

For myself, although I toyed with functional programming in the 1980s, I did not become a functional programmer. Instead, I followed the industry mainstream towards object-oriented programming, and eventually to Java. Nearly 20 years later, Java is, by most measures, the most popular programming language in the world. But, during the last few years, I have not felt complacent about the good fortune of my choice; a programmer who knows only Java would have been missing out on many useful new programming techniques that were appearing in rival languages. Many of these—for example, lazy evaluation, closures, and pattern matching—have their origins in functional languages. And this trend continues: functional programmers are optimistic about their future, above all because trends in hardware manufacturing technology and costs mean that massively concurrent systems are the future. Data immutability will be the key to reasoning about such systems.

Java is not about to become a functional language, but Java programmers should be able to take advantage of some of the insights that functional programming has developed. The changes of Java 8 are a first step in that direction. They bring immutability and lazy evaluation into practical Java programming and so address part of the great and ongoing challenge of partitioning tasks over multiple processors. Despite the commitment to backward compatibility that makes any change to a 20-year-old language so difficult, the Java design team has shown impressive ingenuity in integrating the ideas of functional programming into a language designed on very different principles. They have made a great success of this, the biggest single set of changes in Java's history.

I am excited about these changes, and I hope to have conveyed some of this excitement to you. I hope this book has helped you to understand Java's new direction and, looking further, to become engaged with the future of the language. For the present, I would say this: programming should always be enjoyable, but you will find it much more enjoyable when you are writing the concise, readable, and performant code that Java 8 supports. I would be delighted to think that this book had contributed to making that change in your programming life.

Maurice Naftalin
Pune, August 2014

Index

Join the Largest Tech Community in the World

 Download the latest software, tools, and developer templates

 Get exclusive access to hands-on trainings and workshops

 Grow your professional network through the Oracle ACE Program

 Publish your technical articles – and get paid to share your expertise

Join the Oracle Technology Network
Membership is free. Visit oracle.com/technetwork

@OracleOTN   facebook.com/OracleTechnologyNetwork

Reach More than 700,000 Oracle Customers
with Oracle Publishing Group

Connect with the Audience
that Matters Most to Your Business

Oracle Magazine
The Largest IT Publication in the World
Circulation: 550,000
Audience: IT Managers, DBAs, Programmers, and Developers

Profit
Business Insight for Enterprise-Class Business Leaders to
Help Them Build a Better Business Using Oracle Technology
Circulation: 100,000
Audience: Top Executives and Line of Business Managers

Java Magazine
The Essential Source on Java Technology, the Java
Programming Language, and Java-Based Applications
Circulation: 125,000 and Growing Steady
Audience: Corporate and Independent Java Developers,
Programmers, and Architects

For more information
or to sign up for a FREE
subscription:
Scan the QR code to visit
Oracle Publishing online.

Beta Test Oracle Software

Get a first look at our newest products—and help perfect them. You must meet the following criteria:

- ✓ **Licensed Oracle customer or Oracle PartnerNetwork member**

- ✓ **Oracle software expert**

- ✓ **Early adopter of Oracle products**

Please apply at: pdpm.oracle.com/BPO/userprofile